The
Queen's Decree

FIND PURPOSE, PASSION AND PROSPERITY
YOUR WAY

by CARRIE-ANN BARROW

ISBN: 979-8-9861697-0-5

Dedication

---

*For my Mom and Dad. Thank you for loving me with all
you have and for showing me that it's never too late to grow.*

*For Michael, my King, my best friend,
and my greatest support.*

*For Veronica, the most royal Queen I know.
Thank you for letting the brilliance of your crown shine
its light for others and for always believing in me.*

*For every Queen and King I've coached.
You are the reason for my work. You inspire me and
fulfill my Vision of an amazing, anything-is-possible world.*

The book reflects the author's present recollections of experiences over time. Regarding coaching clients, coaching is confidential and has been respected and honored in this book. Unless the individual requested otherwise, names, characteristics, businesses, and places have been changed and used in a fictious manner, some events have been compressed, and some dialogue recreated.

Table of Contents

Introduction

*"Build your dreams or someone
will hire you to build theirs."*
—Farrah Gray

That simple quote that I discovered while mindlessly scrolling through social media brought me to a halt. It reminded me of something I had forgotten – choice. Whose dream was I building? I read it again and the question kept coming back. Whose dream was I building? Was it mine, my clients', my husband's? Whose?

I read it again. Despite the past thirty or so minutes of comatose Instagram scrolling, I was fully awake in the moment, even a bit shaken. That statement, simple as it is and only 11 words, is what a life well-lived boils down to.

Every intoxicating success. Every challenge you've faced. Every glimpse of growth. It all comes down to this moment – this life-changing decision.

Are you currently building *your own dreams*, or are you building someone else's?

And in the terms of the regency-building adventure you are embarking on – becoming Queen of your own kingdom – *are you going to wear your crown or polish someone else's*?

See, I've been in your shoes. I've been a working professional, a supportive wife, and a loving mother for decades now (but if anyone asks, tell them I'm 42). And for full disclosure, I've changed spouses on the way, but let's save that for later. Before I took charge of my career, I was desperate for change, blind to my incredible strengths, and paralyzed by fear of the unknown.

But I did it. Farrah Gray, the amazing entrepreneur and author of that life-changing quote, did it. Oprah Winfrey did it. Sophia Amoruso (#girlboss) did it. And *you*, you can do it too. You can decide today to build your own dreams, your own kingdom, and not someone else's. This may mean building your dreams as an entrepreneur or bossing up your work life, so you feel more in control of your path, your workload, and your overarching happiness. But what matters is *it's your call,* and no one else's.

To set us on the right path and for you to get the most out of this book – here's what you need to know about me. I'm frank in my communication, resolute in my boundaries and headstrong in my Values. At 40, I lost my filter and have no plans of replacing it. I've built and sold a multi-million-dollar IT consulting business, lived from the profits from rental properties, and today help professionals achieve a level of greatness they never thought possible. Oh, and I do whatever the hell I want. (And I'll help you get that way in no time.)

It's easy to read about others' success, or even mine, and think "They got lucky!" or "Must be nice, but that'll never happen to me." When it comes to self-loathing, doubt, and insecurity – been there, done that. I've battled an eating disorder, dysfunctional family, and other mental health barriers that many of you have faced during your lifetime, too. But I grew from it. I learned, I experienced, and I prospered. Today, if you choose to begin building your own dreams, you'll prosper, too.

"Build your dreams, or someone will hire you to build theirs."

Take a second and really sit with this. Close your eyes. Count to ten. Breathe deeply and clear your mind of the clutter; the unforgiving to-do lists; the immense pressure of work deadlines; the billionth time running back and forth to soccer practice. Recognize the invading thoughts and allow them to go on their way. Or kick them out if you have to. This is "me time."

And then, consider the question – do you want to build your dreams, or someone else's?

When it comes to work, what's most important to you? The safety and stability of building someone else's dream at a reasonable wage, or the encompassing freedom and overwhelming joy that can come from building your own dreams.

It's sad but true – many of us have hired ourselves out to people, societal standards, and belief systems we've adopted as our own without ever really checking to see if they aligned with what was true to us. We took things at face value, without much investigation or soul searching.

We've performed for a salary that meets our surface needs. We've performed to send our kids to the right schools. We've performed to show our parents we could meet their expectations. We've performed to prove "him" wrong. We've performed to drive a car equal to or better than our neighbors or to impress our clients. We've performed to show the world that we can meet its standards of anything from wealth to beauty, to "wokeness," to popularity. But what are our individual standards? How much of the world's standards *even matter*?

Ugh! We perform. We perform. We perform. Often to no applause by the way.

We achieve one goal – not for ourselves, but for our boss, colleagues, family, and personal commitments – and then set the next bar higher, never really processing if it's what we want or what we've been conditioned to believe should happen. Imagine, for just one moment, that climbing that ladder didn't matter.

What if you were satisfied with making less money but had more happiness, time with loved ones, time to just do nothing *but simply be*? What if you had a six-figure job that was sucking the life out of you, and leaving it meant giving up a lot of what the world tells us is important? What if you weren't paid for a few months in order to create longer-term wealth for yourself? What if you decided to be a lower-paid, yet blissfully happy, used bookshop owner, and loved it? Would that be acceptable to you? To your neighbor? To your mom?

Okay, that was a ton of questions, but it all gets down to the same point – what if? What if you chose, today, to do something for you?

What happens next changes everything.

You could decide to become an uber-friendly retail store clerk – downsizing your expenses and reducing the pressure that comes with your multi-level home and obsidian-black Lexus. You could choose to astronomically disappoint your parents by leaving their preferred field, or take a non-profit job that comes with reduced income, but lots of personal reward. You could decide to go back to school full-time and completely change careers, despite being sought-after and offered high-paying positions in your initial career. You _could_ do anything, and that's the beauty of it.

And what I've found is that in my happy place, the money comes. I'm more confident in asking for what I'm worth and creating my income instead of earning it. (I'll address that later.) There are no guarantees, ladies, but I tell you what, I'd rather take my chances on what I can make possible, instead of trading my hours for dollars for someone else's profit line.

What if, as a mother of a toddler, you created a plan for your own dream and left a stable, guaranteed job to risk starting your own business? I did it. I gambled on myself. I decided that I wanted more. I put myself in charge of the odds. I decided to be the House. Queen, Take-the-Damn-Risk, at your service.

What if I told you that each person I just described was a Queen in her own right? Someone who knew what she wanted and decided that it no longer made sense to care what you or me or anyone else thought.

I'm not suggesting anyone quit their job or make life-altering decisions without clarity and a plan. God no, please don't do that. What I'm suggesting is that you open yourself to the possibility that you can be empowered to make your own choices, and that the currency of happiness isn't always green (aka dolla' dolla' bills, ya'll).

This is a tough pill to swallow for most of us – as we've voluntarily jumped right into the rat race. And once we reached a challenging speed, and no matter how hard it was to get there, we pushed even harder and faster because the race, the competitive pressure, surrounded us and it was all we could see.

We ran, sometimes getting to a happy place that lasted a few brief moments or perhaps a few months but was never truly fulfilling. But where have we been running? And how have we not gotten there yet? Was it the act of running itself that became the goal? Was it to a destination that deeply meant something to us? Does it still mean something to us, or has that running become merely a habit? These are questions I want you to ask yourself. Seriously, sit down, and do this. Deal with the hard, emotional shit now. The best is yet to come.

If you're anything like I used to be, you're anxious, overworked, tired, and frustrated. You're angry. Perhaps on the verge of complete burnout. As women, we have overperformed for more reasons than we can count. Except for one – *we underperform for ourselves! How is this okay?* As time has passed, we have forgotten that our dreams, our deep personal desires, and our identities are an essential part of life and a beautiful part at that.

We work hard to get the salary, the title, the house, the next job, but don't focus on what we want in a way that honors what's most important to us. *And we're tired of it.*

If any of this rings true for you, keep reading.

Ladies, it's time to recognize and realize your dreams. It's time to be in charge and make them a reality. It's time to do work for yourself, on yourself, and on your desires. It's time to build according to *your* plans. *And – it's time for a promotion.*

Regardless of the title you may have at the office, no matter what roles you play at home and in life, it's time to claim the title you've already earned - Queen. Queen of your kingdom, your life, your dreams!

Read that quote at the beginning again and cement it in your brain: *"Build your dreams, or someone will hire you to build theirs."*

Are you ready to build?

As Queen Elizabeth I famously said – *"I will have but one mistress and no master."* Now it's your turn.

The best part of this process is *you're* in charge! This is your life that you're designing, and the choices are all yours. And Queen, imagine yourself in all your royal stature with a pen as your scepter. It shows your power, and you'll use it to declare your Royal Decree.

You hold the pen, you make the rules, and you determine what peak performance looks like. You determine the Values your inner Queen needs to honor, your daily responsibilities in taking care of that beautiful mind, body and soul of yours and the skills and tools you need to be successful. This is the job that will get you out of bed every morning. This is the *dream job – and it's yours for the taking.*

In this book, we're going to get to know your inner Queen and learn to give her full attention, ask her meaningful questions, and bring out her boldness. We're going to talk about how to show up with Queen confidence, and how to put her in charge of your life. Not just your job – your life. Because we care about more than work around here.

When you take the position of Queen – Queen of your kingdom, and Queen of your choices – you will know how to synthesize and live your Values, your Vision, and your Velocity (the three magic V's) unapologetically, doing what you want and getting what you're worth.

Your time is now, and this moment is yours. Now that you're here, where you go next is up to you. The first step is sorting through the negative self-talk – about what you can't do and can't have – and finding the lies. Throw. Them. Out.

We're going to lay our path on the truth. The truth is that _you are powerful_. And you, you are in charge.

You can control your perspective, and what Vision does and doesn't serve you. Happiness is sweet; fulfillment is rich. Let's explore how to have both. You've survived 100% of the shit life has thrown at you up until now – that's quite a record, you Badass! You have everything you need in you already.

This is _your_ life. You've been the Queen all along – and it's your time to get royal.

Chapter 1

I Present to You, Your Crown

There's a reason Beyoncé is called "Queen B."

I mean first of all – *look at her*! She exudes confidence. When she speaks publicly, she commands attention. Her wardrobe shows she's thoughtful and intentional in her appearance and understands the impact it has on both fans and foes.

When it comes to interviews, she presents herself with professionalism and positivity, even when it comes to uncomfortable topics. On the Today Show back in 2007, Beyoncé addressed her haters dead-on:

> "There were people who didn't like my first album. There will be people who won't like my next album," she said. "And that's just human nature. I can't expect everyone to love everything that I do. Some of the criticism was constructive and I listened to that and grew from it."

Between her well-put-together appearance and the way she presents herself in interviews – it's hard to imagine a time when she wasn't treated in a way that demands respect. But even Bey deals with haters, just like the rest of us.

Both you and I can wear designer clothes, own a luxury car, perform exceptionally well at work, and even present ourselves in a way that says, "I've got my shit together." But that doesn't mean people won't shit on us. Case in point – let me take you back to a memory of mine from the mid-2000s.

"Excuse me, ma'am," the stout, suited man said to me as he thrust his arm toward me. I could tell he was disinterested. His eyes scanned the room while he spoke "at" me. Caught off-guard, I looked down to see a tan trench coat folded neatly over his forearm which was pointed in my direction.

I was standing at the entrance of a conference for business owners who were interested in bidding on an Information Technology (IT) contract. It was years ago, and back then I was an entrepreneur – the same as today, though I've since switched gears to focus on coaching rather than IT consulting. We'll get to that part of my journey later.

On the day of the IT contract conference, I was dressed in a sharp, black suit with a crisp, blue button-up shirt underneath. My smoothed locks sported fresh blonde highlights. I was a CEO, and dressed the part. I was looking around for one of my business partners who was to arrive at any minute.

The man-with-the-coat's arm remained extended. I looked down at his trench coat, and up. He finally made eye contact, extended his coat further, with a look of exasperation and irritation on his face. Realization slowly crept over me – "Oh, fuck, I get it. He thinks I'm the help."

Despite wanting to snatch his coat and literally light it on fire in front of his face, I simply said, "I'm here for the conference and waiting for my business partner."

Deep breaths.

He didn't appear embarrassed in any way. Unapologetically, he turned his gaze from me and walked in. Without a word.

At that moment I realized that no matter what, there will always be people who will look at me and make an immediate judgment. *What I do* with that moment – not what they do – is what's important. When my male colleague arrived, I told him the story. His eyes got wide, and he burst out laughing.

"Did you smack him?" he asked. I did not. Want to guess what I did instead?

I went on to win that contract.

No matter what you do, where you work, where you live, and how you spend your free time – the world will try to tell you that you are a round peg that goes into a particular round hole. They want you to smile and sit quietly, to dress a certain way and use a particular fork. (That's a personal pet peeve of mine – why the hell does anyone care which fork I use? Seriously, I have better things to worry about.)

It doesn't matter what the world or anyone else wants. The world, your judgmental aunt, your one-upping neighbor, that person giving you the side-eye in a meeting, boiling with jealousy – they are not the Queen of your kingdom, your life, your work, your Values or even your goals. Only you can claim that title.

I'll say it again. You are the Queen of your own kingdom – no one else's – and you are whatever you want to be. Oh, and you can change that at any time.

Today, right now, I want you to own this concept. *You are in charge.*

Both you, me, and all the rest of the women out there – you run the world. You're Queen of your choices, your actions, and your mindset. And no one can tell you any different. It's time to pull out that crown, dust it off, and put it smack-dab on the center of your lovely head.

When I need to summon the strength to rule my kingdom – that woman, my inner Queen – is there pounding stilettos as she walks to the front of my mind, going for what *she* wants, unapologetically. She's empowered, determined, and driven, and you don't want to mess with her.

When I need a major confidence boost, I repeat to myself something like, "Straighten your crown. You are the Queen, and you are killing it." It may take a few repetitions, hell, maybe even two dozen, but I eventually hear it, I feel it, and I believe it.

So, I ask you, "Where's your crown, Queen?" If you don't have an answer, try this on for size. Repeat to yourself, "Right here, bright as the glorious sun blinding all my haters and clearing a path for me!" And if you're not there yet and you really want it, I sure-as-hell promise you will be.

Finding your inner Queen is simple but executing a lasting Queen mindset will take work and commitment. I tell my coaching clients that the real work happens in between sessions. If they put in effort and energy, it'll make a world of difference. Similarly, the real work isn't in reading this book, it's the actions you take after you've turned the last page. It's not enough to know and think about what to do – you must actually do it.

Here's how we go about working as a team to help you along – there are exercises throughout this book for you to complete and tools for you to try. Some of the exercises are to prepare you to step into your majesty; others will become a part of your Queen's Decree. Save your notes, as you'll come back to them in the upcoming chapters.

Ready to step up, Queen? Ready to do the work? It's all that really matters. And I guarantee – do the work, believe in your royalty, and the results will open doors you never dreamed of.

Let's get started by preparing you for this life-changing, sometimes-trying, but regal, all-worth-it ride! Know that you are not alone in this journey. Here are some steps that will help create a successful alliance between us:

Step 1: Trust the Process

First, I need you to trust me, yourself, and the process. Trust that I have nothing but the best intentions for you. Trust that you are the reason this book was written. You are. Like my coaching clients who spend time with me, I want those reading these pages and spending time doing so to become the best versions of themselves. This is what I live and breathe, and I am here for your transformation.

Know that not all stories and exercises in the pages that follow will resonate with you. And that's okay. Not all things are for everyone – remember, you are Queen of your own kingdom, and no one else's. What I want you to do is ignore the examples you don't like and work through those you love. Make time and put in the practice.

Without practice, you gain knowledge but won't build strength, and resilience.

Trust yourself. Trust that you already have everything you need inside of you. Trust that you are brave. Trust that you are ready. Trust your inner Queen. She is there with all of the knowledge, strength, and courage necessary – attributes that will help you clear a path to purpose, fulfillment, fun, and a whole lot of freedom. Trust that you already have what it takes.

Trust that as you go through the process of finding and claiming who you are, you will stay the course. Trust that when we're done, when you are asked "Where's your crown, Queen?" you'll respond, with a head held high and whatever bling serves your inner Queen – "Right here!"

Now, I know it's hard to figure out who you can trust – especially when you're pursuing a successful career and well-balanced, personal life. And I get that. No one deserves your automatic, unflinching trust, even me. So, know that every word in this book, and everything we discuss, is part of me working hard to earn that trust.

At this point in my career, I've worked with clients from their twenties to their sixties, from all walks of life, from high-level government leaders, to physicians, to administrative assistants, all needing to take ownership of their life, their goals, their work. I've made even the most doubtful of them come to terms with their inner Queen or King. It's your job to keep an open mind, and my job to prove to you how and why this works. And I'm damn good at my job. You'll see.

Step 2: Be Curious

Second, I need you to become very well acquainted with curiosity. I want you to be devilishly curious about yourself. Be sneaky. Watch yourself when you least expect it. Be fascinated with what makes you tick, what you do over and over, even when you wish you wouldn't. Be captivated by what you don't do that you wish you did. Record these things, write them down and learn from your behaviors. I'm serious.

Learn what you do, believe, think, and feel that serves you. Along the way, learn what doesn't do you any good. That deep insight, that knowledge, and self-awareness will guide you to fulfillment, as you learn what is most important to you, what makes you tick, what makes you feel fulfilled. It will happen and I'm here to help you. You're badass and strong – and you can do this.

Step 3: Take Out the Trash

Third, I want you to envision judgment as a big, heavy, dirty bag of trash. Or perhaps imagine it as your ex's last box of shit they need to take out of your house right-the-hell now. Now, imagine taking that trash bag or box, placing it in a bin, and watching the garbage truck scoop it up, pull it into the belly of the vehicle, mash it in the compactor, and drive away. Watch it go. Let. It. Go.

It's tough to be curious about yourself, or anything when holding that dirty, stinky bag of judgment. And don't fool yourself. Judgment about others is judgment about oneself. Curiosity and judgment can't coexist. If you're here, you need to lean into curiosity and stop judgment from taking any more of your brain space. It doesn't pay rent; it destroys your inner palace – that beautiful heart and soul of yours – protect it. That judgment isn't welcome here.

Step 4: Write It Down. I Mean It.

Last, prepare to take notes along the way and I'm going to guess you feel some judgment sneaking in – eviction notice delivered STAT. I know, I know – you've been told a million times to journal.

It's therapeutic, offers clearing of thoughts and emotions, and has quantifiable health benefits. Blah. Blah. Blah. But truly, it's your mental way of clearing the crap and focusing on what matters. And it works. I have found that immensely true – and hope you will too, soon.

I want you to write it all. Even the things about yourself that you hate – get it out with pen and paper and if it helps, shred it, burn it, whatever you want when you're done. Set those thoughts free – both those you want to free to fly, and those you want to free to exile from your brain. Journal it! You won't believe how this practice can transform your thoughts.

If you think journaling isn't for you, then don't journal in the traditional way. Write a book or research paper. Make a Vision board. Post sticky notes all over your bathroom mirror or back of your closet door. If you're able to tap into curiosity and ditch the hell out of that judgment, you'll find there's a fascinating topic to address right now – you!

Most importantly, and the "why" of why you're here – you're going to take that fascinating topic and write a Queen's Decree designed for you. A bold declaration about you, a royal Queen. A declaration about what is most important to you and your vision for your kingdom along with other declarations to remind yourself to stand in your gorgeous royalty with your crown of jewels beaming your brilliance. It's a no-BS, the Queen is in the room announcement.

This Decree makes absolute that you are in charge, the authentic you, the "you" that shows up fully, boldly and in your most brilliant, beautiful, messy way of ruling your own kingdom. This Queen. She is here. Now, she may be hiding, so let's ask her to come the hell out. Please and thank you.

Queen – this is your time and it's your turn. You are accountable to yourself. Now that you're equipped with the mental fortitude to shake things up, let's get to it.

Chapter 2

The Kingdom's Foundation

Artists create masterpieces. Entrepreneurs scale businesses. And Queens – well they construct kingdoms, don't they?

You and I both know that Queens aren't *literally* constructing kingdoms. (Though now that I mention it, I'm envisioning Queen Elizabeth II in a signature pastel suit, laying stone at Windsor Castle – and that picture is hilarious.)

The physical parts of constructing a kingdom – laying roads, erecting buildings, and delivering utilities –that's done by hired help, or in the worst-case scenario, indentured servants. As you can imagine, we prefer the former, and never the latter, as we don't rule our individual monarchies that way around here.

Either way, it's a fact that Queens have loads of help along the way.

Now, to construct your personal kingdom, you need help. That's where I come in! But every choice, every decision, every final say, that's all you. No matter whether you're seeking to gain control of your personal life, professional life, or both – *you're in charge* – and it's my job to either help you gain that control or teach you to leverage it.

Case in point – meet my client, Julie.

Julie, a PhD and proud mom of three, serves as a mid-level manager at a large government organization. Her role requires physically demanding hours and a mentally exhausting workload. Every. Damn. Day.

And let's not get into the challenging internal politics at her organization (and when I say "challenging," that's an understatement – her work environment was nuclear-waste toxic). She showed up on my virtual doorstep overworked, stressed out, and struggling, big time.

The immense overwhelm was killing her – the best of us would flounder in that scenario – and it made it near impossible for Julie to identify what was going wrong with her life and how to fix it. She loved some aspects of her work and home life and absolutely hated others.

And when you're drowning under the massive weight of a storm that big – where the hell do you go to escape it? For the record – the bar, a donut shop, trolling your ex-boyfriend on Insta – none of those are good answers. I'm all for knocking back a whiskey or two, but we'll need you 75% sober to start making lasting changes. It ain't easy!

Julie started our first coaching session with a big, warm smile on her face. She cheerfully explained how she wanted coaching to help her with time management. Everything about her said, "This gal's got it together." I used to act this way when I was hurting, too, and I desperately wanted to pull away the professional façade and rip open how she was truly feeling so she could start healing.

I asked her to give me her current assessment of her satisfaction level with time management and where she wanted it to be. She ranked it at the lowest possible, a one, but wanted it closer to seven or eight. She said that it couldn't be a ten because she understood that at this early stage of life, at only 36, she had to put in the hours and build her credibility.

I followed up with, "Okay, so you rated your satisfaction as a one. What does a 'one' look like? Describe your typical day."

Her eyes half closed as if not wanting to see the picture in totality, she took a sharp inhale, and an even longer exhale, before she began: "I set my alarm for 5:30 a.m. so that I can get up, get ready and get dressed before I have to wake the kids. While they get dressed, I cook them breakfast. That's really important to me – that we sit down and have a 'quality breakfast.' I get them off to school, then get myself off to work. I get home around six, then it's time to make dinner. This is assuming no one has any practices or rehearsals or after-school things. We eat dinner, then it's time to get the kids ready for bed – their bedtime is eight, so there isn't a whole lot of time between dinner and bedtime. We have to give them baths and all that. By the time I'm done reading them stories and tucking them in, I give my husband a quick rundown of my day, he does the same, and then I prop myself in bed with my laptop to veg out on 30 minutes of trash TV before passing out from exhaustion."

She stopped, looked down, and finished her story looking punched in the gut. The smile that started the session was gone – and a wounded woman was underneath. I understood. She was productive, organized, and doing it all, but it was a grind (cruise control set at 100 miles per hour) and not the life she wanted.

I said, "Your body language tells me just as much about your day as your words. Now, let's think about what a seven or eight looks like. Describe that day."

Before she even started to speak, I could see Julie's eyes fill and the tears welled up. She wanted to get to know her children, not add them to the to-do list that had to be completed before getting back to work the next day. She wanted off the ever-moving hamster wheel; to feel something other than anxiety, guilt, and disappointment.

She needed to make a choice – a smart, solid choice – and take control of her life, her family, and get to the root of what this Queen wanted for herself.

Choices are complicated because they involve people – you personally, and those you love. People are complicated as are our relationships, problems, families – you get it. In coaching, it often *takes six months or more* for clients to start to really understand what is deeply important to them. And this is essential to reaching a higher level of self-awareness and making actual change.

Let's have this sink in for a second – six months or more. All that time, all that effort, just to identify your deepest and darkest, or brightest desires. We as women are so used to pushing ourselves further past the brink that we lose ourselves. That cruise control Julie was experiencing – time to turn it off. And getting yourself back, and gaining that control of your kingdom, now that takes time. And effort. Know that before you start off on any inner self investigation (whether you're supported by a coach or going solo), it takes time. And that's okay! You, Queen, are worth all the time and effort it takes (virtual high-five here).

With major life transformations – going from the role of obedient good-girl to Queen of your kingdom – there is no timestamp. And we don't want a final destination, after all. This is life! We want to keep moving on a path of our choosing for as long as we can.

Ever heard of the word "Kaizen" or seen it on a motivational poster? In Japanese, Kaizen means continual progress. And that is the path we're embarking on, together. Go on, drink the Kaizen juice with me. And while you're at it, take off the pressure, Queens, and lean into this process! Love this process. Or pretend it's play, and you'll start to witness its positive impact in no time.

And Queens – it's important you know – we are building a whole damn kingdom together starting now! Moving forward with plans and building. It will take time. Be patient, and repeat this with me now, say, "I do not look back!"

"I do not look back!"

Let's do this again – say it out loud for the people in the back (seriously, shout with me now), "I do not look back!" Do that as many times as you need to in order to leave the past behind. The past is for shitty exes, uncomfortable medical procedures, or disappointing experiences with bad bosses. Leave the past behind because we've got work to do.

When it comes to the past – learn it, love it, or at the very least appreciate it, then leave it there. Take only the lessons with you, not the events or replays of an event that no longer need to occupy your brain space. When I have a client that continually talks about a wrongdoing either done to them or by them, I ask them for permission to help them process through it, so that once it's done, it's done. It's a place of feeling through acknowledging, not liking, or finding it acceptable. It's about being able to recognize that it happened and then detach.

The opposite of processing is recycling. When we recycle, we bring the pain, the anger, the wrongdoing back to its original state over and over again – what we didn't like in the first place. We do not need to recycle our wrongdoings or those of others – that's living in a state of victimhood. When we process, we accept what happened and we accept that the feelings associated with it happened as well. We reflect on the lessons and gifts from the experience to make it useful. When that processing is done, we kick it out of whatever room in our brain it was occupying.

Evict it as though you're Catherine of Aragon kicking Henry VIII straight out of her life. She never had the chance to, but you do, if you put in the work.

I spent years second-guessing my choices about everything from my first marriage to job choices, to how well I negotiated my salary, to how I raised my kids, to where we lived, to the outfits I wore, to the things I said (AGH!) – and I hated it. Every single minute of it. No more.

Those were moments. Moments of time. Small lessons. Big lessons. No losers, just lessons. I take the lessons and move forward. I do not look back.

What's done is done. You start now. Your new job is *Queen of Your Kingdom* – and we'll shape it together. Through my experience cultivating my own kingdom and helping others do the same, I find it best to simplify just about everything. Keep it simple, sweetie.

To help you take control of your life in an easy, yet impactful way, I designed the Three VPs Model for Kingdom Building and General Badassery (ha!) – or simply put, the "Three VPs."

Where Values, Vision and Velocity Meet Purpose, Passion, and Prosperity

Values Help Determine Purpose

The term Values is heard around the coaching world, and in short, they are what is most important to you. Sounds simple enough, right?

Not so much! This phase of work often brings about tension because you have to do some honest-to-God inner discovery here to help you determine your true purpose in life. Some raw deep discovery. This aspect of your personal development and purpose-finding takes work, but with time and practice, it gets easier.

You have to determine if the Values you claim are truly yours. Otherwise, the Values are likely those you've unknowingly assumed from your parents, societal constructs, or other outside factors. We often internalize repeated messages and then mistake them for our own thoughts or beliefs without challenge or explanation. You wouldn't believe what I thought were my "Values," decades ago, only to find out they're archaic Values from my parents' parents' parents that no longer serve me and led me nowhere near my actual purpose as a person. My recommendation? Let it all go and do not look back!

Think about it – that repetition, the daily practice of letting negativity go and focusing on the future, on what is meaningful to you – it's as basic as the most sophomore marketing techniques. As a professional ad agency, you wouldn't air a commercial just once and then call it a day, right?

You air the commercial again and again and again. (I'll be honest, though. I'd pay real money to stop seeing those stupid-ass commercials for Poo-Pourri. If I have to hear, "Spritz the bowl before-you-go and no one else will ever know!" one more time, I'm quitting TV for good.)

Expert marketing and advertising professionals know – you want customers to hear your slogan over and over until it becomes part of their vernacular. There's a "Rule of 7" in marketing and business that simply states that the customer or client needs to experience your marketing message at least seven times before they decide to purchase. Search for it online, and you'll come up with a million different ways companies have used this tactic.

Now, if I shout, "Just Do It," randomly in a crowd like a lunatic, it's going to be hard to find a U.S.-based, native English speaker who doesn't recognize the trademark. Because of their marketing team's carefully chosen, three-word-phrase, no one is going to associate Nike with couch potatoes. Ever. You hear it, and automatically bring about associations with fitness, focus and achievement. This is what we want to happen to leverage your Values and help you create a path straight to your purpose.

Start paying attention to these messages you hear on the radio or on TV, and observe how many common phrases you recognize throughout the day. Witness how your mind soaks in these repeat phrases and uses them to inform you subconsciously. The brain is an incredible organ, though calling it that sounds like a slap in the face. It's much more than that. Your brain helps you connect your Values with the Vision for your life.

Most of us, if we pay attention, feel it when something goes against our Values. Our Values live at the core of our being. They are our gut. When something goes against our gut, we feel anxious, uncomfortable, or nervous. Start to pay attention to your gut more. Guts are good.

Look for the Value by asking, "What is important to me that is being stepped on? What am I not honoring, not doing, or doing that is creating tension?"

Now, flip it to another strategy to identify how you're already serving your Values so they can serve you. Remember those moments when you felt complete. Really focus on them and dig deep. When did you last feel like you were where you were meant to be? It doesn't have to be a majorly happy moment. It can be a moment when you took a stand. Perhaps you were angry or mourning and stood up for yourself. And you did it. And your gut felt great.

That's another key part of understanding your Values. Values don't equate with happiness. They can help you understand your purpose – whatever is most important to you. In those moments where you were exactly where you were meant to be, doing what felt so right in your gut, what was being honored? Was it your desire for love? Your appreciation for family? Your pride in achieving equity?

Vision Opens Windows to Your Passions

Think of Vision as the picture of what you want for yourself, your life, and your legacy. Once you have clarity on your Values, how can you make those abstract concepts real and tangible in a Vision?

Let's get really visual here. Queen, what does your castle look like? Is it an expansive, ornately gilded palace, similar to the Palace of Versailles? Or is it something simpler – a Medieval castle, perhaps?

Does it have an alligator-filled moat to protect against your enemies? Perhaps fields of wildflowers with tigers playfully rolling around (that's mine – soft and beautiful but ready to swipe a bitch with those claws when needed). Is it a court of loyal and appreciative subjects? What is your Vision for what you want to be surrounded by – and that helps you identify your true passion in life.

To break it down simply and keep the visual theme, when it comes to appearance does your inner Queen come fabulously adorned with expensive jewels and Marie Antoinette-worthy dresses? Or is she more of a boots-on-the-ground type like Joan of Arc? Nothing, and I mean nothing, is off-limits here.

This Vision is yours. And the more you imagine, and envision who you want to be, the easier it is to feel into it. And then, once you understand your Vision in full, it opens windows to the beautiful passion you have for various aspects of this Vision, and how to weave your entire Vision together to create a wonderful life that is uniquely yours.

As you construct your Vision for your Kingdom, you can even dig deeper if you find it helpful. What does your Queen's voice sound like when she's upholding what's important to you? When she stands up for your Values, your purpose – what is her posture, her tone? How loud is her voice? When she's connecting with family, friends, partners, how does that change? Most importantly, how do you see her values manifesting? What is happening in the kingdom?

Queen, you determine how you show up. This Vision is yours – and so is this kingdom. And passion? No one but you can do this work to investigate what heart-warming, time-stopping activities help manifest your life's passion.

In some ways, Vision is more practical than Values. After all the work you've put into being crystal-clear about your Values, Vision can flow because it's fueled by the work you've already done. Values give meaning, clarity, and direction to your life and your purpose. Vision allows that meaning to take a tangible shape and something to feel passionate about.

Velocity Leads to Prosperity – The Way You Want It

Simply put, Velocity is the chosen speed at which that made-for-you kingdom is built – and sets the foundation for helping you make it happen. Note, velocity doesn't mean the fastest speed you can run. It is the speed you choose to run, and the set of tools and support systems available to you as you continue your journey to becoming Queen of your kingdom.

As a coach, I use your chosen Velocity to help stay the course when the going gets tough. Velocity is protecting the work you're doing as a Queen. It's about achieving and sustaining your prosperity.

Understanding your ideal Velocity helps answer the following questions. How do you avoid burnout? How do you keep the energy you need to continue? How do you keep excitement in tasks that bore you, but are essential to constructing your kingdom? When the Queen needs a vacation, how can you do so without losing all the incredible progress you've made?

To be clear, Velocity is not the same as going full-bore into the rat race. It also isn't about keeping pace with anyone – but understanding yourself, your goals, and your path. Part of the trick to Velocity is finding the drive to keep you going, pushing you toward a life of prosperity. This comes from getting on the right path to begin with – which is why we start with Values and Vision.

Velocity doesn't have to be one speed or any type of speed. Remember: you're Queen. You quite literally get to pick the speed depending upon what's most important to you at any given moment – and you own it.

Own it like English royals own their sordid history (or honestly, should own their history, but that's for another day) – with poise, grace, ownership, and most importantly, the understanding that no matter what anyone says, you're in control here, Queen. And don't you dare forget it.

Chapter 3

What the Queen Needs, She Gets

A Queen's Values are like perfect jewels. They are clear, bright, and can't help but be seen.

A Queen loses direction, and oftentimes herself, without her Values.

Now before you go off thinking, "I couldn't tell you my Values off-hand… all I know is I want to be a good person," know that you're not alone. This isn't a bad thing, it just means you need a little help identifying them, and that's okay! Queens support Queens around here.

Prior to beginning my own self-development journey, I never paid deep attention to what was most important to me. I had these screwed-up notions of how I was "supposed to" think, act and feel. And it was all based on my parents, teachers, media, and societal norms that clouded my understanding of who I was, what I wanted, and what my actual, honest-to-God Values are.

But I've since kicked that BS. With time and effort, I started to peel back the layers of what I wanted for my life – and I can tell you, it works. If you can be patient and understanding with yourself, and give personal development a decent effort, you'll get there, too.

Whenever I have a new client seeking change, I start rooting around for their Values by asking, "What do you really, really want?"

I'm serious as hell here – and I'm asking this of you, too. Do you know what you truly, really want, deep down in your core? If not, start by focusing on the physical feeling. I'm talking about that place in the bottom of your gut that gives you stomachaches when things go wrong, and excited energy when it's going right.

Now, let's try again. What do you want? Is it what you've been conditioned to say you want? Is it what you've been told you want? Is it what makes you happy? I'm going to guess, probably not.

People are complicated that way. Remember Julie? She felt obligated to do so many things because that's how she was expected to behave. By identifying her unique set of personal values, and determining how to honor them, she opened the space to flourish. Are you ready to create that space for yourself? Let's do it!

We'll start with differentiating between happiness and fulfillment to get you ready for the deep dive of finding what's intimately important to you. I'm not talking about fleeting moments of happiness like a sugary glob of cotton candy, a candy apple, brownie sundae, those chewy Swedish fish – red only (I could go on, I love a good sugar rush.) or the intense euphoria of falling in love. (Side note – it's literally the worst that our bodies and brains won't let us continue that happy bliss.)

No, we're in search of the real deal here.

Now, know that identifying one's Values never comes without a little royal inquisition. So, let's focus on fulfillment, first. My client Sarah has a story many of us can relate to.

Sarah was an administrator at an all-girls school serving predominately minority females. She dedicated time and energy into being the best role model possible. She had worked hard, earned the degrees, survived divorce and a long list of toxic bosses. She took the position with a huge pay cut to leave the nightmare of her previous position and the manager that came along with it. That's all too common for women in this world. Research published by Development Dimensions International's (DDI) Frontline Leader Project in 2019 found that 57% of employees left their job because of a manager. That's huge.

The COVID-19 pandemic took an emotional toll on Sarah (all of us, really). She was a hard-working single woman in her mid-fifties who had spent the majority of her life raising her two girls solo. I mean that's rockstar material right there, but she had yet to see it.

When we met, her girls were adults and she had been living alone for more than 10 years – jumping from one high-stress job to the next. Over the years, she never actually enjoyed any of those jobs, but felt she needed to collect the salary increases to pay for her children's education and provide a safe home. And she was dog-tired, like waking up from a 20-year-long coma tired.

As she explained it, she was tired of working so hard and feeling that to get ahead, as the proud black woman she was, she had to work even harder than her white cohorts. And let's face it – she was right. She is right: Slate Magazine and other reputable publications have posted numerous articles on this, with studies showing that minority women do work harder than nearly any other similar demographic but are compensated less.

Because of the pandemic, Sarah was working from home full-time. Her girls lived several states away, and she resided in a city that was on a lasting lockdown. She reached out to me for coaching with career direction and the possibility of exploring entrepreneurship.

I knew the minute we first spoke that it was not going to be an easy road for Sarah. I also saw her crown desperate to shine and knew she was ready. We started by exploring fulfillment. What work would make her feel complete – that she was doing exactly what the universe created her to do?

Sarah explained that the forced working-from-home structure had slowed her down. Without the commute, she had more time, and that time was spent alone. As an extrovert who loved to be around people, this was killing her. (Honestly, I felt the same. I wouldn't have been surprised if, with another month of lockdown, I started talking to the plants!) Working from home gave her some space to reflect and spend time on her coaching homework, which was about discovering what was most important to her.

In one of our sessions, Sarah's body language didn't match her verbal language. I could see she was trying to sound positive and enthusiastic, but Sarah's usual energy was gone as she spoke slowly, without moving. She was practically still as she spoke.

Sarah's demeanor was very similar to when I first met with Julie. Someone who tried to put on a happy persona but deep down, she was hurting.

I asked, "Does your face know how happy you are?" She stopped talking and looked down. After a long pause she looked up. "Carrie-Ann, I've realized over the past few sessions that in this new silence and the additional time I've been given, I only know what I do and what I've done. I don't know who I am. Outside of my kids, I don't know what I love."

So many high achievers suffer from a lack of personal identity. Like Sarah, they know what they do, but they don't know who they are outside of their work. They have spent their careers achieving more than many could dream of – but those achievements have often been to satisfy someone else's expectations, or as a reaction to the conditioning of a competitive culture. Assignments were done to get promoted, not to celebrate or to experience deep, authentic joy.

When was the last time you fist-pumped the air because you killed a sales call, wrote your best blog, baked your best cake, or took your best nap (something I deeply love to celebrate)? Whatever you accomplished – did you celebrate yourself?

It's honestly depressingly sad, but true – we work hard as women to achieve a definition of success we didn't create inside our hearts. Rare is the high-achieving Queen who has sat down and asked herself what her own definition of success looks like, feels like, what it really is. What does success mean to a royal like you? What makes you happy and fulfilled? Honestly though, what is happiness and fulfillment in your world?

To get to the heart of Values, your core Values – those which represent the raw, real you – we first need to spend some time with what fulfillment means, and what it takes for us to be authentically fulfilled.

Throughout life, we are bombarded with an incredible number of conflicting messages. As a little girl, my own parents pushed me to study hard and get good grades, but simultaneously sent subconscious messages that intellect wasn't what mattered.

Beauty, being a "good girl", being polite, getting married to a stand-up guy and having a family were what was important. Society isn't any more consistent than my parents. We are told to be tough, but not too tough because we don't want to come off as a bitch. We have to be pretty, but not too pretty because that could be distracting. We have to be smart, but not so smart that we are threatening. We have to be strong, but not so strong that we make a man feel inferior.

I mean, are you kidding me? Our society is screwed-the-hell-up.

This disconnect leaves us in constant conflict, and, like Goldilocks and those three bears, continually looking for that "just right" job, partner, house, and life – but never really finding one that truly belongs to us. It wasn't our definition of "just right" that mattered; it was our parent's, supervisor's, our community's, our industry's, or social media's.

Consider Hatshepsut – one of the few, and certainly the most successful, female pharaohs to rule over Egypt. Do you think this 15th Century (B.C.) Queen gave a shit about what others thought? Okay, so since she's long gone, we'll never know *exactly what she was thinking* without an authenticated journal. However, we can infer, based on centuries of research, that this was one woman you didn't want to mess with.

According to a Smithsonian Magazine article by Elizabeth B. Wilson from back in 2006 (now available online), "Hatshepsut's methods of acquiring and holding onto power suggested a darker side to her reign and character. The widowed queen of the pharaoh Thutmose II, she had, according to custom, been made regent after his death in c. 1479 B.C. to rule for her young stepson, Thutmose III, until he came of age. Within a few years, however, she proclaimed herself pharaoh, thereby becoming, in the words of Winlock's colleague at the Metropolitan, William C. Hayes, the 'vilest type of usurper.'"

This reputable work goes on to say that, "Disconcerting to some scholars, too, was her insistence on being portrayed as male, with bulging muscles and the traditional pharaonic false beard— variously interpreted by those historians as an act of outrageous deception, deviant behavior or both."

This woman is one badass, and I'm here for it.

See, girls today are often raised to be people pleasers. We are taught to be diplomats, to be nice and non-confrontational. I can't count the number of times I was told as a teen, "You're so serious. Where's your smile?" As if every man that looked at me should be greeted with my stunning pearly whites and adoring eyes. Ugh, gross and fuck off.

As a pre-teen, I was serious and often angry as hell. Something inside of me, even at an early age, recognized that the world wanted me to perform a certain way and it didn't work for me. I was feeling the pressure and I didn't like it – and I made sure everyone knew it. Looking back, the acting out, the defiance, it makes sense. At 12 and 13, I wasn't intellectually mature enough to understand what I was feeling. I do now.

Into adulthood, most of us are so busy that we don't even stop and take the time to consider what makes us fulfilled and happy in the first place. We're great at short-term happiness, like buying a rockin' pair of shoes, finding perfectly fitting jeans, sipping sugar-rimmed cocktails, or indulging in a yummy cupcake (or two or ten or twenty) but these are moments in time. Moments like that don't sustain us. We find ourselves right back in the same rut once those moments end.

Some of us create chaos with overbooked schedules so we don't have to think about our happiness or fulfillment (or lack thereof). The "busy-ness" is intentional. It keeps us from looking inward. We've been unhappy for so long; it feels more comfortable putting up with the bullshit than taking a chance on happiness and learning what's on the other side. Let's fix that.

Okay, bear with me for a second, but for just a moment – forget the concept of happiness altogether.

Is it important? Sure. Is it fleeting? Hell yes, it is. With that, I want you to focus on and get in touch with fulfillment. Simon Sinek, the successful British-American author, and motivational speaker, bottom-lined it with, "Happiness comes from what we do. Fulfillment comes from why we do it."

He has referenced that the only way to feel fulfilled is by doing something for someone else. Sure, I somewhat agree – you can experience fulfillment by doing something for others. However, I'm here to say that I strongly disagree that you can't find fulfillment by doing something for yourself as well. I also want you to understand that fulfillment, sometimes, has nothing to do with happiness at all.

I was asked an unusual question while on a cycling trip through Napa Valley in 2019. It was on one of the first nights when everyone was getting together for drinks at the bar in our hotel for some early group bonding to ensure a smooth week. I sat next to a woman named Chia – a small, wavy-haired woman in a maxi dress. We started some small talk about where we're from, what we do, and the simple icebreakers that we all go through to help conversations become more comfortable.

As we chatted, she shared some of her personal experiences in her life and business.

The chat, however, quickly turned from mundane and obligatory to interesting and engaging – as this particular woman was already a Queen herself. She didn't shy away from what didn't work, sharing her failures just as much as her successes. If she was curious, she asked the question – no holding back. And when I asked questions of her, she was brutally straightforward and unabashedly self-secure. I instantly thought, "Yes! This is one of my people."

Not long into the conversation, she looked at me and asked, "What are some of the best things that ever happened to you?"

What was surprising, even to me, was how quickly the answers rolled off my tongue. (This time it wasn't the drinks, Ha!) I said, "Turning 40 and getting divorced."

Her eyes became as wide as her smile. We were both women that didn't follow tradition. Looking back, I understand why my answer was surprising to her. These were not happy times in the traditional sense. Getting divorced sucks. No one gets married to get divorced. And turning 40 is a milestone that makes you face the limits of your body and realize that you no longer fall into the 'young' category – no matter how you define it or how much filler or Botox you pump into that pretty face of yours (and I've had plenty).

So why was that my answer? Because at 40, I was ready to make choices, hard choices, for me. I started evaluating my life and saw how hard I had worked to prove my father wrong about women. I made a living so my kids would have more than I did, and showed the white-collar world that a blue-collar girl could do it.

See the problem? I wasn't doing any of it for me. It was for my dad, my kids, my community. It was my turn to start doing things for myself too and it was so worth it.

At 40, I took my life into my own hands and made the decision to do what I wanted to do. Some of this had started when I was 32, when I sold my first company and spent a stint selling on eBay because I still wanted to make money but think as little as possible. But otherwise, for years I defined happiness by the standards of others, and I was done. I was honoring my core Values and what was most important to me at that point in my life – autonomy, intimacy, adventure, self-respect, and self-determination. I had more clarity about who I was and who I wanted to be. There were things I loved about myself, and things I didn't, and the choices I made were entirely mine.

By paying attention to what was important to me, I was the most fulfilled I'd ever been, and it turns out that those I love benefited. I was happier, and more present, and this made me an intentional mom, colleague, neighbor, and partner. I took the time to listen and I did so with curiosity instead of judgment.

This process, while about you, serves those you love and everyone around you! This means even the most "people pleasing" among us can see the benefits here. You have so much more to give when you show up as a Queen complete and big, taking up all the space you need. Keep in mind, this space isn't taking up anyone else's space. There are plenty of kingdoms to go around and your example shows everyone else how it's done. The space expands as you do. It all comes down to this – what do you really, really want?

Turning 40 liberated me in a way that I never felt before. I got out of a marriage that was slowly and painfully killing my identity and my joy – and I set about satisfying myself. With every Queenly decree I set for my kingdom, I felt relief. The focus was on me, and only me. I deserved it, and you do too.

I felt freed of other people's expectations. It was as though I had been buying into what everyone else wanted and went along with it. Those lessons are hard to unlearn. I was being "the good wife, the good mother, the good neighbor." The problem – it wasn't *my* version of good.

And it sure as hell didn't feel good. I'd heard it said that people make changes when they're tired of their own bullshit. Yep, hand raised! Tired of saying no to myself because of the wants or judgments of others. Tired of holding back on doing things for myself. Tired of my own bullshit and everyone else's.

It wasn't all easy. After the divorce, I lost some friends. I decided that instead of feeling sorry for myself, I appreciated the time we had together and moved on. I learned how to appreciate being fully human which meant accepting imperfection. I learned to forgive myself much more quickly and to keep on going, head held high, with my crown polished.

Tapping into my inner Queen, I could do and say what I wanted without fear of anyone else's judgment. Sure, the judgment was still there, but guess what? I no longer cared. I allowed the Queen to enter the room, not the Jester there to entertain everyone else.

Here, this should help – can you think of a time when you experienced moments of happiness, but it was a fleeting moment adrift in a sea of dissatisfaction? Maybe you had a great evening out with your girlfriends after getting off work from a job you hated. Maybe you felt high after winning $1,500 in the basketball pool at work, while on the same day worrying about your young teenage son who just got suspended for bathroom vaping (hey, it happens).

What about the other way? Can you think of times when you felt fulfilled even if you weren't particularly happy? Perhaps you were long past runner's high and suffering from blisters and shin splints, but, by God, you crossed the finish line of your first marathon. Perhaps your father died, but you knew you'd made amends with him before he passed. Perhaps you got four non-consecutive hours of sleep over two nights in order to finish the project you were working on, but you did it, and it won you the praise and bonus you knew you deserved.

See? See how happiness and fulfillment don't always correlate?

Sometimes, you're lucky enough to have both at the same time. I have a sweeter-than-sugar friend who loves to bake in her free time. It brings her complete joy to blend all of the ingredients together and create, and she's equally fulfilled doing exactly what she feels she was called to – create and make herself and others happy with her desserts.

Know that fulfillment happens when purpose and action meet.

It's when you are doing what you were called to do, regardless of how your short-term emotions react. Fulfillment isn't aligned with being reactive. It's aligned with being purposeful. Spend some time here on this exercise and figure out what's missing in your life when it comes to fulfillment.

This will not necessarily be fun. And it certainly won't be easy. But you are worth it, Queen.

Finding Regal Fulfillment

To dig into your why and what really fulfills you, reflect on the following questions. Take your time thinking through them and realize that this is where real work begins, so don't rush it. You are worth the energy and effort. Please give this a good try before continuing on with the book – it's more important you go slowly through this work than rush right through it.

- When did time cease to exist in a moment and you found yourself in what is called "flow" in Positive Psychology? It is a state where under the right conditions, your area of fulfillment, you become fully immersed in whatever you are doing. Moments when you are unable to be distracted because you are so fully focused. I get this way when I'm coaching a client who is processing an emotion that's difficult for her. In those moments, nothing else exists for me except the client and what she's working through. It feels like a calling.

- What experiences do you remember that were difficult to go through, but at the same time, produced deep gratitude as you think about them? For me, I felt this when I got divorced. It was one of the hardest things I had to do with three children still at home, but I am so thankful I did it. When I asked my youngest, 13 years old at the time, how he felt about the divorce after about a month of separation, he cried, but still responded, "It's about time." With time, we all become grateful for the hard things.

- What Values are so important that you would quit a job if they were violated by your employer?

If it's a challenge to think through your experiences, try this exercise with your favorite movie or Netflix show. (I'll snuggle up right alongside you with a glass of wine if you're choosing "Schitt's Creek.")

Ask yourself:

- Which characters are the happiest?

- What outward signs indicate to you that they are happy? Does the happiness last?

- Which characters are the most fulfilled?

- What outward signs indicate to you that they are fulfilled?

- Are the characters who are happiest the same as the ones who are the most fulfilled?

- Are the moments of joy the same as the moments of fulfillment?

- Where is the overlap?

- Where is the disconnect?

Use your insight from the exercises above to stay grounded as you continue your journey.

Chapter 4

Owning Your Royal Values

What does a Queen care about most?

Her kingdom, of course. That is her prime purpose in life! And as you do the work to construct your kingdom, make a commitment to being a benevolent ruler, particularly to yourself. If your plan is to be a malevolent one, I'd say go find Attila the Hun's ghost and get tips from him, because that type of advice isn't up my alley.

Repeat after me, "A Queen's kingdom is built on the foundation of her deepest Values. This foundation belongs to her, and no one else."

Maria Theresa, who served as Queen of Bohemia (consisting of Austria, Hungary, Croatia, Transylvania, and other countries) for about 40 years in the 1700s was wealthy and powerful. At least we can assume so based on historical records. She had access to glistening gold and jewels, and a great deal of expertly tailored dresses, in addition to what was likely millions of subjects (that's according to the Schönbrunn Group, which manages nationally important attractions and programs related to Austria's imperial heritage).

With all that wealth, prestige, and subjects at the ready, it would have been easy to let power go to her head. But good Queens recognize their power and respect their roles in their kingdoms, which in turn makes them even better leaders. Maria Theresa had access to wealth and power – but still fought to institute reforms that included universal schooling and abolishing serfdom.

When living to their true purpose, Queens care deeply about the place they call home, as well as the people who live there – and they'll stop at nothing to protect it. Queens put their blood (often literally), sweat and tears into crafting a kingdom they're proud to call theirs. And what makes a Queen so committed to her kingdom? It's the fact that it's founded on the Royal Values the Queen, and at times, her subjects, find oh-so-important.

Now that we know the impact of a solid Values system and insight into your purpose – and the difference it can make, let's put in the work to create yours.

One way to determine your Values is through a process of elimination. When coaching, I give my clients an assessment where they pick from a list of Values to narrow down what they believe to be their top five. Then when we meet, we walk through their choices and identify their core Values. Guess what? At the end of this chapter, we're doing it together. Before we get started, consider Pauline's story.

Pauline came to me for coaching in her mid-forties looking to make major changes. At that point, she was working in a mid-level career job, and was at a stage in her life when she desperately wanted more.

It wasn't that she was looking to climb the ladder, work endless nights and weekends, and fight for promotion after promotion.

Instead, Pauline wanted more out of life – both personally and professionally. And after two marriages that ended in divorce, she was also hell-bent on taking charge of her path and designing a life around her dreams, and no one else's.

Pauline, an African American woman, grew up in a home where finances were extremely tight – which isn't uncommon. According to the U.S. Census Bureau data, about 22.5% of Black, non-Hispanic women live in poverty – more so than Black men (19.4%). In comparison, about 9% of white, non-Hispanic women in our country live in poverty as compared to 7.1% of white men. And what's more, U.S. Census Bureau data also reflects that out of the 38.1 million people living in poverty in 2018, 56%, 21.4 million, were women. The vast differences aren't necessarily shocking but reflect the additional barriers Black women face in their career and life paths.

Back to Pauline. During one of our sessions, she recalled memories from back when she was 10 years old. To help make extra money for the family, she would go with her mom and sisters to work at a fruit and vegetable packing plant (which, sidebar, isn't legal under the Fair Labor Standards Act (FLSA) of 1938, also known as child labor laws). During her shifts, they would pull apart the plants, knock the dirt off and line them up in a basket for packing.

From the get-go, Pauline had to work hard her entire life – and there were no shortcuts. That said, here she was, dressed in royal purple, sitting with pristine posture and ready to do the kind of work that would honor her and the life she was ready for. She was done with the heavy baggage of her past, of her ex-husbands, and anyone else that would get in the way.

We started with Values exercises. She started with what I call the "Good Girl List" of Values – those Values that society tells us we need to own in order to thrive and make an impact. Her list included family, trust, spirituality, and a couple more. Now, I have no judgment about those particular Values, but I felt an internal energy disconnect. I knew something was off as she described each Value with as much passion as describing the spoon she used with her soup.

When Pauline finished talking through what she presented as her Values, I walked her through an exercise to try to break through society's bullshit standards on women – and help her really listen to her heart. I asked her to close her eyes and sink into her chair as relaxed as possible – breathing in, breathing out. Once she was relaxed, I asked her to describe her most amazing life experiences. As she began to unravel the tangled knots of stress, she put her hands on the armrests with her feet flat on the ground, a big smile came across her face – a good sign.

I got butterflies; this was going to be good! It became clear to me that she was physically reliving this incredible experience. (Hint, this level of authenticity produces the best results, so if you do the work to identify your Values, prepare to get real, for better or worse.)

She talked about amazing gourmet dinners, time spent on an aquamarine beach in Puerto Rico, expertly crafted cocktails, and dancing. Her head swayed. She talked about beautiful surroundings and fine foods. She also mentioned the house she wanted to buy and how she truly longed for the finer things.

When she opened her eyes, I asked her, "I hear a Value of luxury, is that true?" She burst out laughing and said, "Yes, I am boujee and I love it."

48

The conversation went on to cover how, because she grew up in a home where money was anything but a luxury, the finer things weren't available to her early in life. But dammit, _she wanted the finer things_.

This exercise, which can often leave people with deep, mixed feelings, made her livid. She felt that because she didn't grow up with money, people assumed that she didn't deserve the finer things in life. She was mad as hell at classism. These were wounds from a difficult life, and they needed to be healed.

No matter where she was from, by the time we were done, Pauline knew she was worth it. She laughed and exclaimed, "Fuck off world, I am that bitch that will buy filet with my food stamps." Now, Pauline wasn't on food stamps and quite frankly had come a long way from the lifestyle of her childhood home, but I understood what she was saying.

Luxury was something she valued, and what anyone else thought, didn't matter. Where she came from didn't matter, either. Pauline wasn't looking back. She wanted that for herself and for other Queens.

Our conversation led to more stories about beautiful places and incredible experiences. I could feel the palpitations in the room. She was alive, excited, and experiencing a joy I hadn't seen in her. This transformation was beautiful, breathtaking – like watching a monarch emerge from its chrysalis. (AGH! This is the best part of my job! It never gets old.)

Pauline was a Queen coming into her own and accepting all she had done – with the freedom to enjoy the very rewards she worked so hard for. She started to see her purpose and get a real grasp on what she was meant to do. And there was a decent chance she would do more of that.

Now, when you think about your Values, Queen, do you feel burdened by what is important to you? Are the Values you're listing more of a to-do list, or do you experience the raw freedom and joy Pauline expressed? Do you own your Values without apology?

Without having met you, I could probably describe you, based on the fact that you're reading this book. Let me guess – you're a high-achieving, smart, competent woman – a decade or more into her career, right? Everyone knows if they ask you to complete a task it will be done and done right. If you aren't already there, you are on your way. (How did I do on that, by the way?)

However, when you look at yourself in the mirror, you probably see something completely different. You're exhausted and the weight of your tired eyes shows it. You have no idea why you are doing what you are doing because you haven't stood still long enough to consider the question.

When you think of your Values, think of those that truly matter. Not those that have been imposed on you by your parents, partner, boss, or society as a whole – but those you care passionately about. Values that make all the work worth it.

Nearly all high-achieving women are victims of "good girl" conditioning. We believed that without conforming to a certain set of rules and expectations, we wouldn't have achieved as highly as we did. To be successful, some rules need to be followed. Whether or not this sat well with our inner Queen, we smiled no matter how we felt. We wore a certain kind of clothes, made sure our bodies fit a certain shape, didn't become too loud, received good grades, and earned every gold star available.

It's why I got married the first time. On paper, from all outside appearances, it was perfect. When you saw us out together, it looked like an ideal marriage. A dual-earning couple with kids, a dog, a cat, and a single-family home. We paid our bills; we worked our assess off; and we smiled in public.

But you know what didn't hit the mark? How I felt about myself when I was with him.

Good girls get married to good boys with good jobs, have their two children and a dog, go to board meetings and PTO meetings, close deals, and bake cupcakes for the bake sale – and we do it all with a smile on our faces.

I worked hard at being a good girl. And I'll bet you've been there. I was a good girl – until I wasn't.

In 2006, Washingtonian Magazine named me one of the Most Powerful Women to Watch. Was I thrilled? Sure I was! Did I believe I deserved it? Absolutely not. At the time, I was 33 years old, and I had created a business that was worth millions. I had three children under the age of seven, and, looking from the outside, I had the perfect marriage.

I was mentoring young women and showing the world that you could have it all if you just worked hard enough and didn't let your fear stop you. *Who wouldn't want to be me?*

Well, me, for one! I was not living my actual purpose in life. Towards the end, I hated every minute of it – the pressure, the stress, the lack of authenticity. While building that business, I suffered from migraines 2 to 3 times a week, the kind that force you to pull over on the side of the road to get sick. The stress I put on myself to perform wasn't sustainable. It was killing me, so I sold the business in 2006.

Another decade of soul searching led me to divorce my husband in 2018 and reinvent my life further. By then, I realized the disconnect between the image I was presenting and my true self. My Values and my Vision, and the passion that comes along with it, were not in alignment with my reality. See, it's not just you, Queen. We all go through this!

I'm sure lots of people thought I was crazy. Why would I give up what I had? Why would I walk away from a business that put me on the short-list of successful women in a power city like Washington D.C.? Why would I end a marriage that ticked all the boxes? From the outside looking in, I had everything women are supposed to want.

And nothing my inner Queen wanted.

Things are rarely what they seem. Our "good girl" conditioning teaches us that approval is the end goal. We want to please our mothers, fathers, teachers, peers, and the readers of Washingtonian Magazine. (I mean, I don't even know these people!)

I was living according to what everyone else thought and disregarded the actual rebellion I wanted to unleash.

I remember being 14 or 15 years old and sitting on the maroon carpeted stairs in our two-story, one bathroom townhouse. My father was going off on a rant, angry at my mother or me for any reason he could find, saying that there would never be a woman president because women were, in his words, "second-class citizens." I was fire-breathing *furious*.

He was ignorant and angry, and as usual, drunk. I remember listening to him, thinking, "Second-class my ass. Before I'm twenty-five, I'm going to be more successful and make more money than you ever did." And I have.

Sounds like a win, right? I'm not so sure. It breaks my heart and pisses me off at the same time when I think about those moments. I use them to remind myself that this is why I'm writing this book. There are loud voices everywhere diminishing the bright light within us – even coming from those who love us deeply – yet don't know how to show it, or those who have their own internal demons they can't break free from.

These voices, heard so often and early, become our inner saboteurs. And when those saboteurs show up – those old, false beliefs – that's when I call up my inner Queen. She shows up with compassion for both my father and me. (He had his own parental issues growing up.) She reminds me that humanity is flawed and still beautiful. She reminds me that *hurt people hurt people* and to do my best to not take it personally as a judgment on myself. She reminds me to look deeply with curiosity to discover what's most important to me, no matter which voice in the room is loudest. It's mine that matters. She shows up, puts the inner saboteur in the dungeon, and gets on with her Queenly business.

And by 40, I became a grown woman realizing I could do whatever I wanted. Did it take me too long? Well, I sure wish I could have figured that out earlier, but we all grow at our own pace. You may be reading this and in your 60s', or perhaps you're 30 and coming into your own. It doesn't matter. What matters is that you're here now. Welcome home, Queen.

Okay, Queen, let's get started! Let's discover those deep-down Values that we'll use to build your kingdom. To help you determine what's most important to you, what really matters, I've included a couple of exercises below. As I mentioned, some exercises and tools will work for you and others won't. Try them and see what resonates, then ditch the rest. We are on a mission with no time or energy for things that don't work for your inner Queen.

Discover Your Royal Jewels

Let's think about moments of flow – those times when nothing else in the world seemed to matter. Those moments when you peaked. When time stopped, and you felt inner peace.

- What were the moments in your life when you were the happiest, content, the most fulfilled? Come up with two or three.

- What in those moments made you happy, content, and fulfilled?

- When did you start to feel confident that that experience was exactly what you were meant to do? How did it feel, physically?

- Is there a common thread between those moments?

- Were they moments when you were in control of yourself?

- Were they all moments when you were surrounded by your loved ones?

- Were they moments where you achieved some level of success or received some kind of validation?

- Where were you emotionally and physically during these moments?

- What were you doing?

Once you've considered when you were happy, content, or fulfilled, ask yourself, "What was it that I was honoring at that time?" Also consider, what served you in those moments and brought about your feeling of happiness, contentment, or fulfillment? Those are your Values.

Now let's continue by taking a look from a different perspective. Let's leave the peak of those flow moments and travel to your kingdom's metaphorical valleys.

- What were you doing when you felt most out-of-whack?

- What made you realize that this experience didn't jive with your internal sense of well-being?

- What physical symptoms manifested themselves when you were acting outside of your Value systems?

  o Did you get a stomachache?

  o Did you feel tired or depressed?

  o Did you get irritable?

  o Did you get ill more easily?

- What compelled you to do these things even though they didn't sit right with you?

- o Was it financial gain?

- o Was it for future gain?

- o Was it because this was a hurdle that you felt you had to clear?

- o Was it simply expected of you?

- Was there a common theme to these instances?

Once you've considered these 'valley' moments, ask yourself, "What was I betraying in those moments?" Those are further explanations of your Values.

Whether the exercise above resonated or not, continue on with this one to give yourself a list to work with, or to refine the work you've already done.

Determining your Values isn't always an easy task and oftentimes we need others to help us sort through our own disingenuous self-talk. Using the lessons of the women in this book, take note, and do your best to dig into what is really important to you. If you have a coach, mentor, or a sincere and honest friend to help you walk through the process, enlist their help. Let them know that you need blunt, direct feedback and are looking for evidence about what is deeply important to you.

When you're ready, take a look at the following list. It is by no means conclusive and meant only to give you a start. If you had to narrow it down to the ten words that speak the loudest to you, which ten words would remain?

Acceptance	Enthusiasm	Intelligence	Purity
Accountability	Equality	Intimacy	Purpose
Achievement	Equity	Joy	Relationship
Adventure	Excellence	Justice	Respect
Authenticity	Fairness	Kindness	Resourcefulness
Autonomy	Faith	Knowledge	Responsibility
Beauty	Family	Leadership	Security
Boldness	Forgiveness	Learning	Service
Bravery	Flexibility	Legacy	Simplicity
Charity	Freedom	Light-heartedness	Spirituality
Commitment	Friendship	Love	Spontaneity
Community	Fulfillment	Loyalty	Stability
Compassion	Fun	Luxury	Strength
Competence	Generosity	Mastery	Structure
Comradery	Gentleness	Mercy	Tolerance
Connection	Gratitude	Neatness	Tradition
Consistency	Growth	Obedience	Trust
Courage	Happiness	Optimism	Truth
Creativity	Health	Passion	Uniqueness
Decisiveness	Honesty	Peace	Unity
Dependability	Hope	Perseverance	Utility
Discipline	Humility	Playfulness	Wealth
Education	Improvement	Pleasure	Wisdom
Empathy	Innovation	Power	
Encouragement	Integrity	Privacy	

Now that you have it narrowed down to ten words, reduce your list to five. There's no objective right or wrong here. This is *your* set of Values.

Let's take your list of five, and say you picked Bravery, Generosity, Love, Humor, and Trust as your Royal Values, or Jewels, and give them a voice. Let's take those words and define them. They are the strong and clear foundation of your declaration, your Queen's Decree.

For example:

> *"In my Kingdom, I value Bravery when faced with challenge, Generosity in support of the less fortunate, Love of all people no matter their station, Humor in the face of strife, and Trust in my court and relationships. The life I have created values these things above all others. When there is a choice to make, I weigh my options based on how they measure up against these Values."*

But of course, words are squirrelly little creatures. They can mean different things to different people. So, let's make sure we've defined our Values according to our own definitions and our own rules. Two of my core Royal Jewels are Autonomy, and Intimacy. I define them as follows: "Autonomy is doing whatever the fuck I want to do and in my own time. Intimacy is being intentional and present in my relationships both with others and myself, allowing space for curiosity and possibility while withholding judgment."

Note that we are not looking to the dictionary to define these words. This is your list of core Values, your Royal Jewels. I've said it before, and I'll say it again – this is your personal set of Values.

<u>You are the Queen of these Values and your life.</u>

It's not the right of Webster, or Oxford, or Dictionary.com to define your Values. You get to define what you want however the hell you want to. That's what freedom is. The only rule is that you make the rules. Live by these Values, and die by them (dramatic, I know, but nonetheless true)!

Chapter 5

You, Dear Queen, Are Beautiful

My Dearest Queens – in this chapter, I share intimate details about navigating an eating disorder. If you choose to not read about it, I respect your decision wholeheartedly, and ask you to move on to the next chapter.

Women are taught that to be valuable, we must be beautiful, and it's never been truer, particularly for young girls dealing with the intense pressure of social media. The reality is we don't have to be a damn thing, but let's go with it for a moment and claim this concept for ourselves. Let's hijack society's plan to make us judge ourselves and compete with one another; instead, let's revel in our beauty and that of others. But to start, we have to answer the question, "What is beauty?"

Let me tell you a personal story about how my confidence exploded as I did the work to answer that question.

I grew up believing that beauty was power, but not necessarily the right kind of power.

Beauty was a tool I could use to get what I wanted from men – my teachers, my boss, the car salesman, a guy interviewing me, a lender at the bank.

My parents, well-intentioned as they were, created this definition for me and I bought it. Mom, all four-foot-eleven of her, was quite a hottie in her day. I remember as a teenager she jokingly told me, "I used to sit on my teachers' laps to get my grades." Ummm, what the fuck, Mom?

She also saw beauty as a competition and had to be on top, even with me. Once, when I was 14, I made the mistake of judgingly questioning her blinged-out LA Gear shoes. (And seriously, ladies, those shoes were so insanely bedazzled, it was as if she literally commanded each rhinestone to transform into Elizabeth Taylor.)

She caught my distaste and immediately became vicious, declaring, "If we went to the mall and both dressed up, I could get more boys your age than you could." After the initial hurt and shock, I remember thinking, "You're right." For a 14-year-old girl, that was quite the confidence blow. Now, I realize it was her own fear of getting old and not being beautiful. Beauty was the one thing that she believed got her through life, and in her mind that was being threatened as she aged.

My mother was taught that her main Value should be her Beauty, and so she believed that mine should be as well. Her Vision for me was a cute little mama, baby on my hip, making dinner for my working husband.

She pushed tight clothing on me, only for me to reject it. I'd shop at Sunny Surplus leaving with clothing two sizes bigger than my actual size because that was how I saw myself and I wanted to hide.

My mother would criticize me, telling me how awful my outfits were and that I should be wearing this or that (and this or that was cut much smaller). I believe that she thought she was being helpful. However, she didn't realize that it made me feel even less attractive. No one had taught her to celebrate another woman, only to critique and compete.

Near the end of her life, my grandmother was watching me help my children with their homework. She commented on the patience I displayed with them. "I'm sorry about how much I yelled at your mother," she said. "I called her stupid. I even smacked her because she couldn't learn how to spell."

Needless to say, I was horrified by what I was hearing.

My grandmother continued. Maybe she knew her time was drawing to a close and this was her time to do some clearing. "I would teach her something, and I thought she'd learned it, but the next day it was as if she hadn't heard it at all. We had to start from scratch, and I'd be so frustrated." I'd yell, "How can you be so stupid?"

Grandma's chest heaved with a big sigh. "It was a good thing she was pretty."

My mother literally learned from her own mother that she was stupid, but she had her looks going for her and that was enough.

So, my mother used what she had – her sex appeal, highlighted to advantage with white miniskirt and Nancy Sinatra boots. When it came her time to raise a daughter in the 70s and 80s, when women were exploring and claiming their worth outside of physical appearance and value as a wife to a man, she had no idea how to approach it. Women all around her were making independent decisions regarding abortion, education, politics, and business.

The times, they definitely were a-changing, but not so much in my blue-collar home. My dad made it clear to me that women existed as wives and companions to men. Anything else was unthinkable.

I was getting mixed messages. My father taught me the alphabet and how to write my name by the time I was three. Every single day he spent hours with me reading. He taught me to draw and was, on many levels, an amazing, involved father to a young girl. It wasn't until I started to become an adolescent and expressed opinions, that things took a turn. As young parents who had their own difficulties in their childhood and who had me at only 21 years old, parenting was a challenge.

Every little offense I committed became twisted into something else. At age 14 when I lied for a friend about sneaking out one night, I was called a "whore." I felt pushed to achieve academically, but was taught at the very same time that it didn't matter how smart I was since I would only be judged by my looks and my ability to be a "good wife."

As a teenager, my Vision of myself was limited by deep insecurities and criticism – and that thrust me further away from my purpose in life than anything ever could. Things got worse as I began to develop. The bigger my breasts grew, the more I just felt, well, enormous. At 16 I was squeezing myself into a C cup. (Seriously, Mother Nature, you're throwing this at me on top of everything else?) I started throwing up my lunch at school and was terrified of getting fat. No one there was watching or had any idea what was going on.

Eventually, my mother started asking questions, and I felt like she was catching on. I would throw up in bags, jars, or any empty container I could get my hands on. I would hide them in my room and then take them out to the trash later. I'll never forget the day I came home from school and my mom was standing in the front door looking mad as hell. Somehow, I knew she'd found my secret.

While she was angry, I could also see that she was confused, even hurt, and didn't understand at all what was happening. She told me she had weighed the vomit. There was over 14 pounds of it. It was horrifying for both of us, and she was lost. She called my pediatrician, who referred me to outpatient psychiatric visits. I went for as long as my parent's insurance would cover it – a whopping three visits. It didn't make any difference. I just became better at hiding my behaviors.

I struggled with bulimia on and off for years. I would be good for a while, but whenever I didn't like the way something looked on my body or, in my twisted opinion ate too much, I would punish myself for eating by hurling it back up.

One day, when I was pregnant with my second son (and yes, still struggling with bulimia on and off – this eating disorder is horrible and real), I decided I had had enough. I was going to love myself.

I was sitting in my car, seven months pregnant and feeling huge. I was giving myself hell for eating so much. It was a ridiculous thought – I was pregnant for Christ's sake! But there was no grace. I was 28 years old, and I had it in my head that I needed to lose weight while carrying a baby. (I know, I know! I can see it now. That was messed up, but I know you'll get it. We've all had life-impacting stressors trigger some unexpected behavior in our lives, though how it shows up isn't as equally awful for everyone.)

Right then and there it struck me. This was a complete mess – and it didn't have to be my mess anymore. I had to love my baby and myself. I was more than numbers on a goddamn scale. And I deserved to eat. The beauty I had been sacrificing my health and that of my baby for was anything but authentic – it was a societal construct taught to me by my mother and bought by me at way too high a price.

My body was mine and that alone was a reason to love it. I wanted to see myself with a new Vision, a new purpose for my family, my work, and my ultimate contentment. I would find a way.

Eventually, I started spending time inside my own heart and mind instead of worrying about how other people saw my body. I started to focus on myself and really dug deep into what was important to me – I was creating a Vision of my life. I wanted to experience Beauty as I saw it, not as what other people saw it for me. I redefined it. To me, Beauty became confidence, both in my best moments and in all of my wonderful moments of imperfection. Beauty was about loving myself. I wanted to be completely comfortable in that space.

It took me a while after my second son was born to be fully comfortable with self-love and to appreciate all of me – but I got there, little by little. I started by clearing my closet of anything that didn't make me feel confident and bought clothing that did. I enlisted the help of department store employees that I thought had style to help me pick out outfits. I started journaling daily affirmations and writing down what I liked about myself.

After I got divorced, I spent a lot of time exploring what beauty really was. It had been such an important concept in my life, but it had been defined and perverted by external forces. I wanted to believe and feel that I was beautiful – all of me, complete with my imperfections.

In 2017, I hired a photographer to get some pictures for LinkedIn and my website. I found an amazing woman named Alyona. As part of her photography work, she interviews potential clients to understand what they want to show through in their images. She began by interviewing me about my "brand" and how I wanted to be seen. She asked me about my life and my career. As we went on, it led to a more personal conversation. I told her about my divorce and how that made me feel liberated. I wanted some of that newly found freedom to show through in those pictures. Alyona, with her creative spirit, asked me what I wanted the photos to say. She was asking for my Vision of myself, the Vision for all of me, not just the "pretty" part.

I explained that I wanted my photos to show all sides of me. I wanted to show a beauty defined by strength and confidence. I also wanted to show joy and the happiness of finding comfort in living in my own skin.

As I've said before, being a Queen is about making choices for ourselves. My Vision of myself was changing: who I was, who I wanted to be, all that I could be, how I wanted to show up, and how I accepted myself. It was no longer my mother or father's version. It wasn't the models I grew up with. It wasn't the pressure I had put on myself as a teen.

Whether it was me in a glam gown and black pumps or in the front of the room leading my company's team on a new project or wearing clothing that showed my tattoos – even the bad ones, or me sitting cross-legged on my couch with one arm around my kid watching Disney movies and sharing a bucket of buttered up popcorn, I was beautiful in whatever role I chose. The confidence was found in the beauty of making my own choices – being whoever I wanted and doing whatever I wanted.

Alyona got it. We took some professional LinkedIn pictures, but we also took some pictures that were just for me. I spent an entire day with her and her stylist, and she captured all of me. Spending time with an incredible artist and investing in myself helped me feel and see all the things I was and could be. She suggested that we do some boudoir shots, something I would not have thought to do. And I am so glad I did. With help, and a lot of encouragement from Alyona, I picked the outfits, the poses, the expressions.

I saw in those photographs that I was my own person – smart, sexy, beautiful, strong, bold, and yes, above all things, enough and happy to be living for me.

Queens, I cannot express what a positive experience that boudoir session was for me. I was making my version of beauty come alive. If you have ever considered it, even for just a moment, make the phone call now and book your session, and don't give me any excuses about age, size, or being shy. You are absolutely beautiful. Let yourself show it.

That smile you see in the boudoir picture? It didn't exist prior to that time. The secret to unlocking that smile was putting myself in charge as Queen of my own kingdom – and I haven't looked back.

Define Beauty on Your Terms

Your work, Queen, is to spend time writing your definition of beauty. Define it by your standards and yours only.

Use your imagination and be curious about how you think of beauty. Bring no judgment with you. I want you to drop all preconceived notions of size, age, and anything that you've been told that defines beauty. Bag it up and with all the strength you have, throw it directly into the trash truck!

Close your eyes and picture yourself in full royalty. Head high, shoulders back, in charge of your life and feeling like you are exactly where and what you are meant to be. You are beautiful. Spend time there.

Slowly breathe in your beauty, feel it. Adore yourself. Tell yourself that you are beautiful over and over again.

If you start to hear other voices, allow the Queen to silence them and repeat it again, "I am beautiful" until you see it and then, describe it. You are the definition. Write it down. This is your definition of beauty. Own this, dear Queen. This is beauty. This is you.

Chapter 6

Your Kingdom Is in Sight

With your Values recorded and feeling hot-hot-hot with your beautiful self – let's discuss that Queenly Vision. This is what opens the window in your soul to a prosperous life that encompasses all of you - health, wealth, achievement, spirituality – all of you.

Throughout a woman's life, her Values are challenged. They're almost guaranteed to change, again and again, as she grows further into the Queen that she was meant to be.

Whether you're a literal royal or a figurative one, know that as you grow, you're going to betray yourself by stepping on a Value or forgetting what is most important to you. As humans, we're imperfect and that's okay. Seriously! We fall. We get up. We try again. Next time with eyeliner – or whatever you need to make yourself feel like the badass you are.

There are times when your old Values compete with your new Values – and this will throw you a curveball the weight of Britain's crown jewels (which Queen Elizabeth II says can break your neck). When you feel the weight of your kingdom pressing against your neck, I want you to have a Vision you can go back to that will re-mind you of who you are and who you want to be. A Vision that is yours, not the world's or anyone else's. Reminding yourself of your Vision, and the passion you have for it, will get you through just about anything life throws at you.

As women, we're many things and _we can be anything_ – so dream big with that Vision and be free in identifying your passions.

This wasn't always true for us. Speaking for women in the United States, we couldn't vote prior to 1920. Women couldn't get credit cards without their husband's signature until 1974 (and yes, I'm shaking my head and asking, "Are you kidding me?" right along with you). Prior to 2015, women couldn't compete for front-line ground combat positions in the U.S. Navy. And that was basically five minutes ago in the span of history. That's mind-blowing to think about, isn't it?

There was a time when _we couldn't;_ we were limited by laws and society's expectations. While we "couldn't" at the time – you and I know that we sure as hell "could," had we been given a chance. As women, we have battles we still need to face on this front, but our Visions can soar in ways they weren't able to throughout history. We're very, very fortunate, to live in this century. So, let's own it.

Queens are rulers and therefore have autonomy. And know that personal autonomy isn't just being in charge of yourself from a legal standpoint. It's far more than the fact that you get to make your own medical, marital, social, and appearance-related decisions. It means that you get to decide who you are and how you express yourself under any circumstance.

Your personal autonomy is what gives you the power to rule as Queen. No matter who your boss is, who your spouse is, and who you are responsible for – you are in charge around here. This means living your life according to the desires and motives that you have designed and created. You have the agency and choice to live a life free of manipulative or distorting external forces that come from culture, poor parenting, social media, and lifelong conditioning. You are no one's serf – you rule your life, your Vision, and your Values independently.

One of my all-time favorite quotes is, "What others think of you is none of your business."

Say it with me now, loud, and proud. Declare and own it, "What *others think of me is none of my business!*"

Think about that for a second. What if we didn't make the opinions of others relevant? What if we made it none of our business even when they wanted it to be our business? That is some Queenly power move right there – and I want this for you! Your Vision for your kingdom, your life, is yours and yours alone – guard it like a Mama Bear!

The Queen's Vision

Okay Queen, it's Go Time!

For this you will need:

- Assorted magazines that you can cut from

- Sharp scissors

- A glue stick or glue Posterboard or cardboard

- Glitter, stickers, or decorative items

- A fabulous soundtrack.

We're going to make a Vision board of the complete you, Queen. All of you – every role as well as how you want to take up space in the world. Spread your materials out on a table or on the floor and get your tunes cranking. If you want, you can do this as a group activity with friends. Go through the magazines and cut out any pictures that speak to all you are and all you want to be. And be creative. This doesn't have to be literal. You don't have to use photos of yourself in different outfits. You can represent your strength, softness, fierceness with colors, or types of animals, flowers, foods. Whatever speaks to your Vision.

Seriously. Don't think about this too hard. And sure as hell don't think about what others might think! Go in with the mindset that you are making a Vision board of the full you and let your instincts drive you. Once you've cut out a picture, glue it on your posterboard or cardboard. And if this still feels overwhelming, then start with your crown. Breathe deep, close your eyes, and take it in. Is your crown gold, silver or something else? What kind of gems adorn it? Every gem can represent something you're proud of – how bright are their colors?

When you feel satisfied that you have enough pictures (or you've run out of magazines), if the mood strikes you, decorate your board with glitter or stickers or whatever suits your fancy. There's no right or wrong here, and you don't have to show it to anyone when you're done. This is for you. There is no judgment. If it makes you happy, it's the right thing to do.

Now that you're done, take a step back. Look at it from a distance. See if you can "read" your Vision board. You might have to put it away for a week and then look at it again to get a real sense of it. What do your pictures have in common? Is there a theme that runs through them? Is there a color that you are drawn to? Is there an activity or a type of thing that keeps coming up? Does it make you aspire to anything?

Without the world judging you or giving you an outside standard by which to judge yourself, this is what your Queen wants to see. And it's goddamn glorious.

We're ready to begin the next step of outlining your goals – the Vision for your kingdom. I suggest that you create goals for one year and create a new Vision Board annually. It's a great reminder of how much life has in store for you!

Jot down on a piece of paper, in full sentences or just scribbles, your Vision for your life and your kingdom for the next 365 days.

Does part of your Vision mean setting healthier boundaries at work so you can focus on your family at home? Maybe your Vision includes focusing more on supporting others by volunteering – because you and I both know you can always make room for your priorities.

When you've outlined your goals, jot down a word next to them that will motivate you to persevere when times get tough. Perhaps, if you're focused on healthier boundaries, your word is "resilience." As we all know, that's needed when people keep pushing, and pushing, and pushing on our personal boundaries. You get the idea? Now get to work!

Chapter 7

From Your Court, Queen

Now that you've got an understanding of your Values and a Vision for your kingdom, it's time to focus on Velocity. We're going to explore the tools and strategies you'll use to manifest your Values and Vision and keep them alive! This chapter and those that follow will support you.

As women, there's a Queen inside all of us – and we welcome her into our lives wherever we see fit.

Do you need to be a badass bitch to ensure you are heard? Call upon your inner Catherine de' Medici – the ruthless Italian noblewoman and Queen Consort of France for about 10 years in the 1500s. Known for her hardline policies and the persecution that was carried out under her son's rule – she was not to be messed with. Now, am I saying you should go out there and create chaos in your own kingdom? Hell to the no. But I am saying that inside you are glorious segments of your personality that you can tap into, and call to be your front line on the battlefield.

At about 45 years old, after my metamorphosis into the magnificent monarch I am today (get used to having confidence, Queens, because that's where we're headed) – I divorced my husband. I tossed him, and yes, nearly 20 years of marriage, straight into the bin, and never looked back.

Shortly after, I ran into a guy I'd known for decades and hadn't seen in forever. "Carrie-Ann!" he said, waving excitedly with wide, warm eyes. "You look fantastic! You look the same as you did when you were thirty-two."

"That's because when I was thirty-two, I looked like I was forty-five," I said.

He laughed like I was joking. Nope.

I suppose it was tongue-in-cheek, but it was the absolute truth. I remember being thirty and going to a business conference for women.

An enthusiastic young woman greeted me and my vice president and made sure I knew that they had groups available for women over forty. Before I got the chance to jump over the table (said in jest, of course, as my inner Queen is a compassionate ruler), my VP leaned into the woman and shared my actual age and a little mentoring about making assumptions.

It's funny to me now and my reaction seems, and was, overly dramatic, but at the time it was devastating. Did I really look that much older than I was? I guess there's only so much you can do to cover up your inner life.

Of course, I am now in my late 40s, and I've earned the right to look it and feel amazing about it too!

Not that long ago, I started looking in the mirror missing my old friends (you'll know who they are... keep reading). See, I had nursed three kids, and my once-perky, bra-filling 34 Ds were now

34 "downs." I'd look down at what gravity (and big-eaters) had done to my chest, and I really, really wanted a boob job. I hated how my girls looked like empty gym socks that I had to roll into a size A bra.

Did that define me? Of course not! But I hated how they looked in a bikini top or low-cut dress. I'm sure some of you are thinking, "Girl, get a different bikini top or try another higher-cut dress." Guess what? I love bikinis and love black-tie events and wanted to look the way I felt – smoking hot and in my mind, having boobs did that for me. You do you.

My ex-husband had been dead set against a boob job, so I never seriously considered it. And the guy I was dating at the time didn't want me to have one either. I spoke to some friends about wanting to get the work done and while most were supportive, I was shocked by a few of the responses including, "You're not 25 anymore. You're a mom, why would you want that?" True, I wasn't 25 and yes, I'm a mom. So what? I'm a lot of other things too – I'm a woman, a leader, a badass, the boss-of-me, and you know it, a Queen.

I wanted my girls back but hadn't made the decision to do something about them because of men in my life and the irrelevant opinions of a few others. I was at a place when I wasn't allowing my Queen to rule. I was giving in to the opinions and wants of others. Until I wasn't.

They were my boobs. Not my ex-husband's, not my partner's, not society's. Did I honestly care if anyone thought I was superficial or silly or stupid if I got a boob job? I wanted my tits to face forward, dammit. I wanted to fill a bra. And why shouldn't I?

I made my own choice. I got a boob job. And you know what? It was one of the best things I've done for myself. After the seriously painful recovery, I felt confident and sexy and proud. Not just because of the way I looked, but because I made that decision. I made the decision for me, and that was empowering. Every time I walk by a mirror and see myself standing just a little bit straighter, I know that I have the strength and the willpower to do what I want to do, no matter who says I shouldn't.

But that's the thing. Perky boobs aren't part of my Values. My Vision doesn't consist of people staring at my chest. The measurable speed of my Velocity is in no way related to my cup size. But what does align is that I value autonomy and my freedom to do whatever I want to do. My Vision is to look up, not down, both literally and metaphorically, with my eyes and with my breasts and posture. Being true to my Values and Vision allowed me to maintain the energy I needed to sustain Velocity.

Put simply, my new tits are spectacular. And so am I. And Queen, so are you.

In order to wake my inner Queen and put my saboteur to bed, I had to hush up everyone else's voice and listen to myself. And I want you to do the same thing.

There's a client of mine, Rhonda, who suffered from mental whiplash, running in one direction, then abruptly changing course. One minute she was working hard at her job, the next she was cooking nutritious meals for her kids and playing chauffeur, then she was trying to maintain her relationship with her husband. She was struggling with the never-ending list of priorities and her saboteur was loudly telling her that she wasn't doing a very good job at handling any of them. She was desperately trying to be all things to all people all at the same time and feeling intense guilt and judgment when something wasn't done at 100%.

"I have no idea who I am," she told me. "Am I a businesswoman? Am I a mother? A wife? A charity worker? A worker bee? A boss? Every three minutes someone wants me to be someone else. All these different roles are competing with each other."

Suddenly, a vision popped into my head. I pictured Rhonda in a classic Wonder Woman pose wearing a pair of those kick-ass, sexy boots. (Well, hello to my next Halloween costume!) A power-red cape fluttered behind her. Now we're getting more visual here – picture this, with her were several Rhonda-clones, her Power Posse. To her left was Madame Corporate. To her right was Mighty Mom. Filling out the crew was the Natural Nurturer and standing boldly in front – her Queen.

"Rhonda, these women inside aren't competing with you – they're your squad of superheroes!" I said, feeling joyous in knowing she was close to a realization.

"What?" She was confused but curious.

"They don't have to work against each other. Those beautiful, and distinct parts of your personality are all allies, not enemies. All those different women inside you are your personal army against pressure, other people's wants, and against the good girl conditioning from your childhood. When your daughter needs nurturing, you send out your Mighty Mom. When there's a project due at work, that's a job for Madame Corporate. When someone has stepped on your values, bring out that G.I. Rhonda to kick ass! They're not tugging you in different directions. They're taking charge of your kingdom on your behalf – and they can also be there for one another to give clarity and direction, and to give one another a well-deserved break. Their sole purpose, together, is your fulfillment."

Whoa. It was like a bomb dropped.

After that, we had so much fun talking about her Posse — her royal Court — making up names for them and identifying the jobs they did. And that was an amazing start, a reframing of the way she looked at her internal conflict, getting in touch with the different roles she played, and who she wanted on the front lines at any given moment.

Rhonda's saboteur was her attitude learned from her own mother who was an extreme workaholic. She had been told that she had to do it all. Over time, that felt suffocating. She would look at a task with the idea that it isn't just one single objective, but multiple, overarching duties. She would fall into exhaustion. When she looked at each task with trepidation, realizing there were 10 more to follow, her energy was drained before even starting. However, when she went to a PTO meeting knowing "Mighty Mom" had it covered with backup from the Queen, she went in feeling empowered and that made all the difference.

This exercise isn't just for moms. All of us get pulled in different directions — whether we see it or not.

We get pressure from our parents, from our friends, from our significant others, from our jobs, from the charities we work for, from the networking groups we belong to, and from the hobby and affinity groups we might attend.

Appoint Your Royal Court

The following can work for anyone who has more than one responsibility or pressure – and who doesn't? Honestly, we're all strapped as hell and all of us can use this practice.

Lots of us have conflicting roles and we feel guilty as a result. We all have our stress. Perhaps it's our aging parents complaining that we don't give them enough attention, the gals lamenting that we haven't had a girls' night in ages, our kids wanting us to babysit the grandkids, our jobs screaming for more time while our significant others demand their due – and when we take time for ourselves, we just flat out feel guilty for doing it. There don't seem to be enough hours in the day. We are always being told we should be doing something else for someone else, and rarely think of ourselves.

Imagine yourself as Queen of your kingdom, looking down from a precipice at the expanse, the bustling towns, and thousands of subjects. You're not just any Queen, you are the Queen, with a glistening gold crown (or silver, if that's your thing), a royally-stunning, purple velvet gown made with expert craftsmanship, your perfectly-coiffed hair barely blowing in the wind.

Think of the different roles you play. Who do you need on your team? Who is backing up the Queen? Who is in the Queen's Court on any given day? Is your Chief of Court available to deal with obstinate team members at work? Is your Keeper of the Privy Purse free to handle financial challenges? Who goes on dates – the Queen's ladies-in-waiting? Who goes to charity events?

If you're feeling artistic, draw pictures of your Court. If you're not, see if you can find images on Pinterest of powerful women, past or present, who will get these jobs done for you. Put them all together into a team for yourself. Come up with names for everyone, and, when you feel overwhelmed, let the right member of Court hop in and get things done for you. They're here to help – so use them!

Chapter 8

Speak Like a Queen

Words matter.

I mean, hell, that should be obvious. You can't just call up your client, parent, neighbor, partner (or anyone, really) and say, "You're a total ass," right? (Well, there may be some exceptions but you get the point!) Instead, you and I both know that we're responsible for the careful word choice and delivery of difficult statements. And the words we choose in difficult situations make or break the relationship we have with the person on the receiving end.

The reason I bring all this up is because now we're talking vocabulary – and I promise not to lecture you on the topic, unless you need a good lecture. If so, call me, I'm great at them. It's time to get some freedom from the words and thoughts that have held you down.

Queens use language that is accurate, direct, and free of the bullshit. For example, Queens don't say "I'm sorry" unless the apology is valid and warranted.

Let's make this practical. Consider the following (sorry, not really sorry) apologies:

"Sorry I haven't responded to your email earlier."

"I'm sorry I was out of town (*when your urgent request came in*)."

"I apologize for missing the party; I needed 'me' time."

Now, if I asked you to collect your most recent "I'm sorrys" and the list above was it – here's some alternative responses:

"Sorry I haven't responded to you earlier."

Are you truly, actually sorry, Queen? Maybe that person emailed a low-priority request when you have a million other things to do that are more important. Maybe your mother called demanding help with her Facebook password when you were working. Or perhaps a colleague called after-hours. Either way, if you aren't actually sorry, you aren't apologizing. Period.

So how would I respond? I would get back to them when I could, apology-free.

"I'm sorry I was out of town (*when your urgent request came in*)."

Oftentimes situations like these arise from poor planning on behalf of the party making the request. Sure, it's your priority to set an out-of-office, or otherwise notify people who may need your help that you'll be unavailable. If you've done your due diligence, in my mind, you've done your end. It's time for them to do theirs.

My response here is "I was out of town when your email came in…" And continue with what was needed *sans* the "I'm sorry." Easy peasy, weazy.

"I apologize for missing the party; I needed 'me' time."

One of my colleagues decided to skip a friend's birthday party, and boy, were they pissed. They made it known that her absence would 'ruin' the fun and she felt terrible for the decision she'd made! But guess what? She's an adult. She can make her own choices, and if she chooses not to attend a party and take time for herself, so be it. If they let her absence ruin the event, that's on them.

My response, "I hope you had an amazing time. I look forward to next year."

Ever notice how you say this at the grocery store, all the time? We'll say, "I'm sorry" for walking between someone and the row of canned goods they are looking at (For Pete's sake, just pick a can of corn and move along.) – when actually, there is nothing to be sorry about. And for women, this is even more pronounced as we're taught that "good girls" apologize.

There's this great study done by Karina Schumann and Michael Ross at Ontario, Canada's University of Waterloo's Department of Psychology. They found that women felt as though they committed more offenses than the male participants in the study, and in turn said "I'm sorry" more than men. That's because "men apologize less frequently than women because they have a higher threshold for what constitutes offensive behavior," according to the study's abstract on the National Library of Medicine's National Center for Biotechnology Information (PubMed.gov).

A second, related study tested the hypothesis by asking participants to remember past offenses that required an apology. And, "as predicted, men rated the offenses as less severe than women did. These different ratings of severity predicted both judgments of whether an apology was deserved and actual apology behavior," the study stated.

This does not look good for women. We have some changes to make, my Queens. By defining ourselves as wrong, we contribute to the perception that we are wrong. We start self-identifying as wrong – and Queens, we will not be having any of that from here on out. Okay?

Take a second to consider your latest "I'm sorrys." What are you tired of saying you're sorry for?

I was recently in Charleston, South Carolina for a dear friend's lovely, intimate wedding. (And I love weddings. It's by far my favorite place to catch up with old connections and make new ones.) While walking along a very busy sidewalk and chatting with my partner, we came across a group of people standing together in a bunch, taking up the entire walking space. (Ugh, I literally hate that.)

As we approached the group, I thought about how I would typically say, "Excuse me," or "I'm sorry" to walk past. I also knew I wasn't sorry and that this group was in my damn way! They were the ones who should be sorry for literally taking up the space of 5 people.

Instead of apologizing, I quickly scanned my mind for a better alternative. As I approached, my inner cyclist kicked in and as I got closer, I announced, "On your left." (It was the best I had in the moment.) I got a bit of a strange look from the group, and then got an apology as they got out of the way. (There was a Queen approaching, after all.) An appropriate apology, by the way! Lesson of the day: don't block sidewalks, dammit.

Now it's your turn. Here's the first part of your assignment.

The Sorry List

Spend a week carrying around a small notebook or keeping a list on the notes section on your phone. Be mindful of your own speech. Every time you use the word "sorry," make a note of it. Then have a space to write down: are you actually sorry? If you weren't, what compelled you to apologize? Did that action really have an offensive impact or is that a story your guilt monster is making up? Is it a habit ready to be broken?

Keep in mind, Queen, I expect this list to be about a hundred lines long if you're in the habit of saying "I'm sorry" for damn near everything. And that's okay! You can't correct your behavior unless you can call it out. Let those unnecessary "I'm sorrys" show themselves so you can kick them the hell out of your life.

It's also worth considering – what new vocabulary could you use instead of "I'm sorry?" Maybe, "Thanks for your patience," or nothing at all?

I'm an "I appreciate your patience" kind of girl. I love that line. I'm never sorry for doing the best I can to respond to friends, relatives, even and especially clients. If someone is making a request of you, they must be patient. It's not like you can walk into the doctor's office and say, "I need to see my doctor ASAP," and then have the front desk step in immediately to clear the schedule for you. That's insane – though wouldn't that be nice. And if you do have to wait for your appointment or call back from your doctor, they sure as hell aren't apologizing.

Now take a pause, craft your list, and come back to continue reading.

Welcome back! You've completed that list, right?

Now that you've identified when you say, "I'm sorry," let's figure out what you can say instead. Start sentences with the substance of what you meant rather than an apology. You do not need to warm up a sentence with an apology. I'm sorry, but you can dive right in. See what I did there?

Here is my most simple advice:

Get straight to it Queen!

Say what you mean, whether in person or in writing. You have business to do and don't need to warm up communication with an apology. As an example, I've heard employees tell bosses, "I'm sorry, I have to leave to pick up my kids," when it's already past 5:00 p.m.

This is your time Queen, and unless staying late is something you've already committed to, no explanation is necessary. You get your royal tush up, say goodbye, and head out the door. If asked to stay later, make a decision, without an apology.

Unfortunately, what I described above often bleeds into non-working hours. As a serial start-up entrepreneur, I understand working late nights and weekends. This was particularly true in the early stages when I was trying to build my client base. I was responding to emails and requests all hours of the night and weekends. The reality is – I wasn't doing that because I needed to. I was doing it out of fear that they wouldn't be there tomorrow.

No more, and ladies – to hell with fear! I still receive emails and requests from potential and existing clients on Fridays at 8 p.m. or on Saturdays and Sundays. I respond on Monday and leave out the

"Sorry I didn't get back to you sooner." Why? Because I'm not sorry. I am here for you ladies – but I'm here for my Values and myself first so that I can serve you at my fullest.

And guess what – I know I'm a hella good coach! Those potential clients will be there tomorrow, and I will kick ass for them in the time I've carved out *just for them*. If you or I were to start the email with "I'm sorry I didn't get back to you sooner" (sooner meaning any hours we define as our own), we aren't giving our inner Queen credit for the fabulous space we give ourselves to refuel our energy and be our best selves.

Once, while working with a client on some difficult leadership issues, she broke down and said, "I'm sorry, I hate this job." And she definitely didn't need to apologize to me. Coaching is a safe place, a no-judgment zone – yet there she was apologizing. I stopped her, asked her what she was really feeling. We explored the feeling from both a head and heart perspective and where it was showing up physically. Sure enough, she wasn't sorry at all. Her body was tense; her teeth clenching. Her stomach was in knots and she was getting hot. What she was feeling was frustration, not sadness, and definitely not the need to apologize. I asked her to stand up and declare what she really felt.

> "I hate this fucking job. I hate the way I'm being treated. I hate the way other women are being treated. I'm done," she said. Once we got rid of the artificial apology, and dealt with what she was really feeling, the work happened.

In your royal vocabulary, you'll find it's equally important to use certain words a lot more. One word, that is actually a complete sentence and that the Queen has full command of, is the word "No."

One of my favorite quotes from Warren Buffet is, "The difference between successful people and really successful people is that really successful people say "No" to almost everything." I Love it! And I personally, want to be a really successful badass Queen! (Thinking that led to me to thinking of Warren Buffet in drag... I'll move on.)

So, say it with me – "No!"

Practice it: "No." "No." "No." "No." "No." Say it in your shower. Say it to yourself when you're being a critical asshole to yourself. And when you've practiced, start saying it to others.

In this kingdom, the Queen unapologetically values her time, her skills, herself and knows that there is only so much of her to go around. Saying "Yes" too much leads to burnout and robs the Queen of her electrifying, beautiful, and powerful energy.

Social psychologist and published author Dr. Susan Newman talks a lot about the power of the word "No." As women, especially, we want to make everyone around us happy. We're taught from the time we are little that pleasing everyone around us is our primary goal. Where we fall down is that we can't please anyone if we don't please ourselves first. Saying "Yes" too often brings on stress and anxiety and poor performance when we're stretched too thin.

Gross. That archaic, 1950s-bullshit could make my eyes roll right out of my head. Know, Queen, that you do not need to say "Yes" all the time. You do not owe anyone anything. Say "Yes" less, and "No" more, and you'll be amazed at the impact this has on those around you. The ones who matter will see this and respect you more for it. Those who don't see it don't matter.

One more thing to note about vocabulary. The words others use with you is also important. An example in my work is while working with a male client, he texted me that he would like to discuss an issue before our next coaching session. He also added, "And I would just like to hear your voice." (Um, red flag! Retreat!) In my twenties, and even thirties, despite that my gut reaction was "This guy needs to back off," I wouldn't have said anything – "No worries," or "Happy to help." I don't do that anymore. These days, I have a full Queen Vocabulary List and I use it.

Back to this client. His language crossed a boundary for me. Instead of using the vocabulary of silence, at our next session I said, "There is something I need to discuss with you. When you sent this text and added that you would just like to hear my voice, it came across to me as flirting. As your coach, I want you to be the best version of yourself and I believe that you see women as peers. Regardless of your intent, that is not how this text translated to me."

As his coach, I am his mirror reflecting back an image of himself that he may not be able to, or perhaps doesn't want to see. We talked about his vocabulary and when I explained it to him, he was horrified and had no idea it came across that way. I learned that he was brought up in a traditional household and his language mimicked that of his father. It wasn't so much that he wanted to be that way or had even thought about it – it was that he had no idea that he came across to me in a way that I found inappropriate (and he wouldn't have had I not told him). He found my voice easier to understand than my emails and was completely ignorant to the "gentleman" vocabulary he'd been taught to use. That day, we made a commitment to work on his vocabulary and other-awareness.

One boundary I have with clients is I am not responsible for the work they do between sessions. I hold them accountable to their goals. My job is to help them discover new perspectives and use the resources they already have internally, as well as develop new tools to be their greatest selves. My Queen-worthy job is to do the same for myself. By honoring my Values and my boundaries, I took a stand on what's important to me – how I am treated by my clients. By doing so with the best intentions for my client and myself, we both benefited. This can apply anywhere – in your work, your life, your relationships.

You have your Sorry list, now move on to the second part of your assignment.

Address Opposing Realms with Your Royal Vocab List

This work gets me going! No matter where you come from, how you were raised, and what your social interactions were like in your past – you're here to grow and focus on the future. We're going to do the work of undoing our "good girl" socialization.

Imagine you're five or six years old in elementary school and there is a Queenly teacher standing tall with confidence in the front of the room. Make it someone you look up to. Perhaps it's the former first lady Michelle Obama up there. Maybe it's Olympic award-winning gymnast, Simone Biles. O.M.G. – I adore that young woman and her amazing confidence in saying No at the Tokyo Olympics!

For me, it's Cindy Eckert, founder of Sprout Pharmaceuticals, a company that helps women address hypoactive (low) sexual desire disorder (HSDD) and low libido. She also founded The Pink Ceiling, a philanthropic firm that invests in groundbreaking companies that are improving healthcare for women. She's a female entrepreneur who proudly declares, "I want to help make women really fucking rich!" How can you not love her?

Now imagine that she's giving you a vocabulary assignment. It starts with making a list of "good girl" words you use that are sucking your energy and then develop a new vocabulary to protect it.

I've included a few examples below to get your list started and left some rows blank for you to complete. Once you've finished your list, create an example of how you can see yourself using it in the future. And then – practice, practice, practice! Use your journal to create as many as you need.

Old Vocabulary	New Vocabulary/Action	Practice Examples
"I'm sorry"	Apologize only when truly sorry.	Thank you for your patience. Say nothing at all.
"Yes"	Read Warren Buffet's quote again. You are "really successful people" so simply put, say "No."	Yes! "No," I don't have time for that additional project. Yes! "No," a 6 p.m. meeting doesn't work for my schedule. Yes! "No," I won't be going to the office happy hour.
"But"	Sometimes, "But" can be misconstrued as an apology. Try using "And."	I'm excited about the new project "and" I'll take my time as I go along to fully understand the new skills I need. I would love to go to dinner with you "and" I'll be a little late because I have to take care of a few personal things.

Old Vocabulary	New Vocabulary/Action	Practice Examples
"Silence"	Silence can manifest as approval. If you don't agree with something - set boundaries.	I enjoy having you over "and" it's important that we both have enough energy for the next day, so let's end the night by 9 p.m. (See how we have a bounce AND used the word "and" instead of "but.")
"Just"	"Just" is minimizing. I "just" need a little more time. I'm "just" doing my job.	The deadline isn't realistic and I'll need another week. I've worked hard. Thank you for noticing.

Chapter 9

Royal Resiliency

There are monarchies that move at the speed of light.

Alexandrina Victoria, known as Queen Victoria of the United Kingdom of Great Britain and Ireland, reigned from 1837 to 1901. That's a whopping sixty-three years and, at the time, it was the longest rule of a British monarch (though Queen Elizabeth II has surpassed her).

During her time as Queen, Queen Victoria spurred the great expansion of the British Empire, and became Empress of India in 1867. By the late 1800s, her empire covered one fifth of our earth's surface. Her rule was so effective that her reign became known as the Victorian Era.

She's the kind of leader that makes me desperately wish ghosts were walking around this earth so I could haul her into a conference room and pick her brain. If she were here today as a successful entrepreneur, she'd give Arianna Huffington a fantastic run for her money (that would be one of those moments where you pull out the popcorn bowl, ladies, because that would get so, so good).

Queen Victoria knew how make things happen. She used what she had and leveraged her resources. She chose to move with exceptional Velocity – and that's what we're exploring today.

See, Velocity is that inner, deep-in-your-belly drive that pushes you when you feel as though you can't go any further. It's what helps you wake up in the morning excited about the day and the possibilities that lie ahead.

Maintaining that drive can be really hard. There are days when I want to hide in my cozy bed, sheets pulled over my eyes and escape from the world. We've all been there at some point or another – but it's Velocity that breaks you from that pattern and propels you towards productivity.

Remember when we were kids, about five or six years old, when you'd wake up, pop out of bed, and be bursting with energy and ready to play. Now, as we get older and our daily activities get more and more out of alignment with our own Values, Velocity slows down and makes it more challenging to get through the day. Our minds and bodies naturally fight against pursuing work and completing projects that don't match up with what our heart really wants and yet we fight back and do it anyway. Here's a cup of burnout for you…and you… and you. It's time to say, "No thank you!"

When you're deep in the thick of things, it's hard to realize how bad things have become – so I use my energy level as a metric to help me stay the course. When I can no longer "wake up and go," something is wrong – really wrong.

That means I need to take a look at my Vision and Values and focus my energy on crawling out of the hole. If you're in that position, there's no reason to get down, seriously. I know that feeling of being lost, detached, and desperate is incredibly awful – but there are ways you can get through this. I've done it multiple times, and you can too.

Queens can't afford to be knocked down for long – because we've got work to do. A couple years back, I had this incredible client Joanne who was experiencing a devastating divorce. And it pissed her off to no end that everyone she knew seemed to be falling all over themselves with sympathy for her soon-to-be ex. "Poor Joshua," they'd say. Meanwhile Joanne was thinking, "Fuck that, he did this to himself!" Her friends and family expressed deep concern of how he was going to manage on his own.

She once told me, "I'm having to figure out how to manage on my own, too! It's absolute bullshit and unfair. I'm tired of my mind frantically spinning every night when I attempt to go to bed. I'm losing sleep and I'm losing sanity. Why can't anyone feel bad for me?"

I knew how she felt. I went through the same thing when I got divorced. It felt like every time my ex-husband managed to shower and put his shoes on, he got an 'atta boy' and a heartwarming hug, whereas I was expected to do everything alone with strength, independence, and fortitude.

I said, "Joanne. It's because you're a high achiever with high standards, and you make everything look so easy! You don't drop balls, and you'll go days without sleep and self-care to make sure you don't fail, and all the projects get done. And you'll do that while you're baking cupcakes for your kid's class, taking the dog to the vet, and doing your makeup at red lights in the car. It's incredible. And you're incredible but it's not sustainable."

Joanne just laughed. "It's like you have a camera following me around. I'm just so fucking mad. I'm busy doing everything for everyone and he's busy acting pathetically helpless," she said.

"And you aren't. This is such a blessing. But that doesn't mean you can – or should – do everything."

"You're right," she said. "I just want everything to be okay for my daughter and I don't want her to see me having a hard time. This divorce is already so hard on her."

"She means the world to you," I replied.

"Yeah…" Joanne said with a pause. "I want her to know that this divorce isn't about her. It's about her Dad and me, and that I'm going to do everything I can to keep things the same for her."

"But, are they the same?" I asked. "What is she learning as she watches this process?"

Joanne thought about that for a minute. "I don't know," she said.

With her eyes softened and focused on the floor, she went quiet for several minutes. I waited. Work was happening in the silence. She took a deep breath, and responded, "She's learning that Mom does everything and Dad just sits on his ass doing the bare minimum. I don't like what I've taught her – and that's changing. She needs to know that she shouldn't be expected to do everything. That she doesn't have to be perfect. I want her to see, from me, that it is okay to disappoint other people in favor of giving herself a fucking break."

"That's an empowering lesson." I added, "The problem with making it look easy is that when it isn't easy for her, she's going to think she isn't measuring up – similar to how you feel."

Ugh, that was a rough one to get out there. Joanne stared, looking like I'd punched her in the face.

"What if you admitted to yourself and everyone else that it's not so easy after all," I asked. "What if you said 'No' to some things?"

Her eyes widened, and I could see her energy levels already increasing with the thought of releasing some of the weight she'd been carrying. With her warming to the idea, we sat down together and created a "fuck it list" aimed at giving her the space she desperately wanted (and a break from the chaos of doing it all).

When we started – and I'd bet my paycheck this is where you are starting, too – everything Joanne had to do was, metaphorically, in one of those giant Rubbermaid totes with handles that she could barely lift off the ground.

I'm guessing you've been there. Here's what's true though Queens – you have a life to live and gorgeous mountains to climb with amazing views waiting. And you can't do that while carrying the baggage of societal expectations, or as I did for too long, the baggage of grown-ass men. (Oh yeah! I carried it too – the heavy psychological baggage of my ex-husband – but that's another story.)

Queens, as women, we're always carrying more than our load. Hell, that's expected in today's world and it's time to make some serious changes. We all deserve better.

Like Joanne, it's time to unload your overflowing tote and separate it out into three buckets:

1. The Keep It Bucket
2. The Delegate Bucket
3. The Fuck It Bucket

Ready to get started? Think of this as closet cleaning. Put your things, your responsibilities, your projects, and your assignments into three piles – keep (Keep It Bucket), donate (Delegate Bucket), and toss (Fuck It Bucket).

You'll find some things are wonderfully worth keeping. And there are some things that waste precious space in your house (hell, your mind) but they'd be a treasure for another. And there are some things that are just so useless they need to be pitched out the door.

To determine what to keep, compare your "to-do" – those responsibilities – with your Vision. Take a second, align it with your Values and see if the "to-do," the task, the job is a good match. If it connects and feels right, you'll know.

Now if you find a task doesn't align with your Vision and Values, become curious and more honest with yourself. Where should it go? It takes a bit of time and effort – keep at it – you've got this!

When Joanne and I were finished, the only bucket she'd still be carrying around would be the Keep It Bucket, and she could lift that, no problem, with one hand. Yes, Queen! We all have the right to a manageable load – whether we have subjects to handle the weight of the rest, or if we want to off-load it completely. With a little strategy and determination, this can be you.

To be frank, this is no small task, though. Joanne's instinct was to put everything in the Keep It bucket. (I've been there more times than I can count.) Like most high-achievers, Joanne knew what she was good at, and she felt that if she wanted something done right, she had to do it herself.

Here's the thing, though. Let's assume that's true. That Joanne could do the things on her to-do list better than anyone else. I challenged her. "So what? Do all of them have to be done to perfection?"

Sometimes, good enough is, well, good enough. You might bake the best upside-down pineapple cake on earth, but the one at the local bakery is good enough for the dinner party. You might put together the best PowerPoint presentations, but your intern's PowerPoint presentation is good enough for an in-house team building exercise.

Joanne was best served by saving her talents and energy for the things that really needed them, not what wanted them. Some of the things didn't need to be done at all. Sure, it would be nice if her daughter had a hand-made Halloween costume, but the one from the store can be just as good. Better, maybe.

Remember – just because you can, doesn't mean you should. Chuck it in the Fuck It Bucket and move on. Your gifts and talents are needed elsewhere, Queen.

You can use this same method for anything in your life. One of my clients is a physician. She was working up to 80 hours a week (holy shit), doing all she could to give her patients the best care possible – and in the rest of her time, trying to give her family just as much. She wasn't, however, taking care of herself. It was an unsustainable pace. She was exhausted and miserable and wanted a way out.

We took a white board and put three circles on it, each representing the buckets we described above. For each "to-do," we separated her tasks into the Keep It, the Delegate or the Fuck It bucket.

It wasn't an easy process: as we worked together, she redesigned her life. It was powerful to witness. We shuffled a few things between buckets. In less than a year (after more than twenty years of working insane weeks), she went from working 80 hours a week to 35, making the same money and at the same time regaining her power. Hell, talk about a transformation!

For another client – it wasn't about the hours she was working, it was about the *unpaid* hours she was working. Heather was a full-time employee in a large organization making what appeared to be a solid six-figure salary. However, what started at 40 hours a week, became 60, then 70, and then weekends as well. You could see her life force was being sucked right the hell out of her.

It was a slow sink downward over a couple of years, and that became the norm. By the time she found me, she was totally burnt out. What was surprising was that the hours weren't the biggest issue for her initially. She was demotivated when she realized that, after dividing her pay by her hourly rate, she was being paid a lot less than she realized. And that is an experience many of us women have faced in the past – and it's devastating.

Her Vision was actually quite simple – to be paid for every hour she worked and to be paid what she was worth.

One of my favorite Peloton instructors is Robin Arzon. Now there's a Queen! You can't help but be inspired by her story of leaving a high-paying industry to do what makes her happy. If you don't know about her, look her up and take her classes! Her crown is bright ladies, and she uses it to create light for others. She inspires me to continue to polish mine. One of my favorite quotes from her is "Know your worth, then add tax." Yasssssss! Heather was ready to do just that!

Heather and I got to work and spent a couple of hours with the three buckets. There were tasks only she could do – ones that she sincerely wanted to do. There were tasks that she delegated to others, and then there were the things that weren't necessary.

She came to peace with the concept that "Done is better than perfect" and got the work done without agonizing over it. And was paid. By the time we were done, her Queen was front and center, crown held high. She was taking back her most precious resource, her time, and getting paid for the time she was giving to others. She was building her kingdom. Hell yes, Heather!

This practice – the Fuck It Bucket challenge as I call it – helps determine your Velocity. You give your energy where it is needed most so you have enough in reserve to keep going. For Heather, unpaid labor – such as organizing the company's holiday drive – had to go in the Fuck It Bucket, even if that meant a few side-eyes, or gossip from the people who expect you to do it again this year. Sticks and stones may break your bones, but side-eyes will never hurt you. In fact, with the right mindset, they are empowering.

Now, it's your turn to fill your Fuck It Bucket! No seriously, we're doing it. Just as you'd dump that god-awful fashion from the early 2000s, (Who thought deeply low-rise pants with 'Bootylicious' on the ass were ever a good idea?) you're going to toss the dead weight from your life – and feel lighter, and happier.

I know you're thinking, "I'll just read this chapter and think about doing it. Actually, it sounds like a lot of work for now, so I am going to keep reading."

Hear me loud – Queen, put your crown on, show up, and do the work! This is your time to take charge. If you act with intention, it is going to make a much bigger impact than if you just think about it in the abstract. Do professional golfers just read about their swing, or do they get out there and hit buckets of balls? This is a rhetorical question. They hit buckets of balls, obviously. And you, my friend, are going to hit some balls too (now ladies, I mean this figuratively, ha!).

The Bucket-Emptying Ceremony

This exercise will help to keep you grounded and aligned with your Queenly Vision. Get out of your chair, your bed (wherever the hell you are), and get some paper and a pen. Or fire up your laptop and open up a spreadsheet. If you have access to one, stand next to a giant whiteboard, (Nothing says productivity like a giant-ass-whiteboard.) or one of those big paper pads on an easel with fat markers in a tray below. Better yet, you can use huge sticky notes you can paste across the wall. Now those are fun.

If you're more of a literal person, get three actual buckets and label them "Keep," "Delegate," and "Fuck It" to ensure you're treating yourself in a Royal, and just way. Make sure there are no small children around who are learning to sound out words because I will not be held responsible when your child starts acting like the badass you are.

When you're ready, list everything you can think of that is on your to-do list. List big things like filing taxes and completing the quarterly compliance report with the regulatory agency – really, whatever it is you have to do. Then, add small things like dropping off dry cleaning and getting pens from the supply closet. If you are using the actual buckets, put each of these tasks on a separate piece of paper. If you want, you can do this twice, once for work stuff and once for home stuff, but let's be real – it's all one big messy plate from one big messy buffet table, isn't it?

Queens have to rule their kingdom, but they also have to lead their households. Why pretend you can keep things separate?

Next up, symbolize your buckets. If you have actual buckets, great. If you are using a spreadsheet, label columns. If you have giant sticky notes, label one of each. If you have a whiteboard, draw big circles. Blah, blah, blah, you get the idea.

Then one by one, go down your list of tasks and put them in buckets. What do you absolutely, positively have to do yourself? What can you get someone else to do for you? What doesn't really have to be done at all? (Side note: you'll notice during this practice that you do a hell of a lot of things you shouldn't, but don't let it get you down. This is necessary to lift you back up!)

When you've completed your first go-round, look at your buckets. Which one is the fullest? Likely the Keep It. Is there anything at all in the Fuck It Bucket? Look again, what's in the Keep It Bucket? Surely there is something in there you can delegate?

What's in the Delegate Bucket? Does everything in it really have to be done? Seriously, Queen, time to be honest with yourself.

Write out that task on a piece of paper if you haven't already done so; hold it in your hands. What would happen if you just threw it in the Fuck It Bucket and it was never done? Who exactly would be mad? Would anyone even notice? Would the earth tilt off its axis?

I'm the last person to say you aren't important. You are extremely important. To you, to your loved ones, to your children, and to a select group of friends. But the truth is that for most tasks we complete, we are interchangeable with any number of people who are perfectly capable of completing that same task. That doesn't mean you aren't a wonderful human being.

Let's face it – it's a little bit arrogant to presume that only you or I can do things in a way that produces an acceptable outcome. Don't you think?

Being attached to a particular outcome and a certain method to reach that particular outcome might, in fact, be the best way to guarantee failure. Things rarely go the way we plan them. Being flexible allows you to go with the flow when things go in unexpected ways. Refusing to become wedded to one particular outcome allows you to celebrate unexpected success.

Anyone with reasonable competence can be trained to operate a lawnmower, or cook a nutritious meal, or work through numbers on a spreadsheet. Do you really presume that you are the only competent person? Just because the lawn doesn't look like it would if you mowed it, the meal isn't quite as delicious as you would have cooked it, and the graphs on the spreadsheet aren't as pleasing to the eye, none of that means that all of those things aren't done competently. They're just not done the way you would have done them. And that's okay. And yes, I know you're feeling extremely called out right now and That's. The. Point! Queen, you're getting your life back on track. It's hard as hell, but you can do this!

In conclusion – to HELL with control. Put "control everything" in the Fuck It Bucket, stat, and start giving yourself the Royal Treatment.

Chapter 10

The Royal Treatment

A critical part of Velocity is self-care, or more appropriately named here, the Royal Treatment.

As I wrote that I couldn't but help picture ladies in waiting, horse drawn carriages, and others attending to my every whim. Personally, that would get old and isn't what I'm talking about, but for a few moments, it's a welcome thought.

The Royal Treatment I'm talking about is what others can't do for me – the actions and choices I make to ensure my mind, body, and spirit are well, and that they are given the attention they deserve for me to show up fully and enjoy all that life has to offer. The Royal Treatment is about giving myself permission and encouragement to make myself the priority.

Having grown up in a family where self-care looked more like self-medicating, I had no early role models for a healthy lifestyle. My dad's version was alcohol. My mother's version of self-care was buying shit, and then buying more shit. This, of course, would lead to a cycle of my father losing his shit when the boxes just kept coming. It was the mid-80s, The Home Shopping Club was a "thing", and it was her thing! My childhood consisted of school, listening to my parents arguing about money, watching TV, and visiting Grandma on the weekends.

And oh, how I loved going to my grandparent's house! I have amazing memories of my grandmother baking cakes, making noodles from scratch, and doing whatever she could to make me happy. Those weekends were bliss for a young child, but not what I would call lessons in self-care. I remember the constant request, "Care (short for Carrie-Ann), go get me a beer." And I can't forget the cigarette smoke being so thick in the house that my little brother and I made a game of army-crawling under the thick haze. It's funny, yet so not funny, to think about those moments. We had fun crawling around under cigarette smoke, coughing our little laughing heads off and smelling like Marlboros when we left. Good Lord!

Over the years I would play with the concept of self-care in dabbles and drips, primarily focused on the physical. My screwed-up version of beauty didn't help in the early years. It wasn't until my early forties that I really started to pay deep attention and go beyond physical self-care.

My divorce pushed me to pay attention. I had invested so much into trying to save a marriage that was already dead, that I had forgotten about investing in myself. During the final, worst years of my first marriage, the old lessons from my family came flooding back and alcohol became my self-care. I started to go out with a girlfriend who was single and stay out until two and three in the morning. Sometimes my teenage kids would be awake when I got home – that was the worst. It wasn't pretty but I couldn't see it at the time, and it went on for a couple of years.

I finally had my "time to wake-up" moment when we had good friends visit, a couple I adored, and I couldn't spend time with them because of a horrible hangover. They drove a good distance to be there, and I couldn't get my ass out of bed. I needed to make some changes. The self-care journey started and shortly after, I told my husband that I wanted a divorce. I was miserable in our marriage and the self-medicating wasn't working. This was the start of living for me.

Self-care looks different for everyone; however, it starts with making yourself relevant and sometimes, making other things irrelevant. As I went through that divorce, there were things that would really trigger me, and I would be tempted to fall into old habits. I realized that this was happening because I was still making my soon-to-be ex-husband relevant in my life. One day, after he had moved out, I got the mail, and his name was on one of the envelopes. That was it. All it took was seeing his name. I was filled with rage. I'm talking fire-breathing rage. How dare the mailperson put something with his name, those simple letters put in the most offensive order, in MY mailbox? I was going to chase down that damn mail truck and shove that letter right up....

Oh. My. Fucking. God. Wait Carrie-Ann, I thought. What the hell is wrong with you? Why are you giving this so much energy, so much power? Why are you still making him relevant? Something had to give. Think Carrie-Ann, think. I closed my eyes, gripping that envelope and for some reason, thank you Universe, an image of the word *relevant* appeared and then the two letters, "I" and "R" floated in and were placed in front of the word relevant. As simple as it sounds, I decided to give myself the gift of the "I" and the "R". The letters, I decided, stood for I Rule. And when I rule, I make the bullshit, including my ex-husband, irrelevant.

I can't tell you how many times I used that thought to get me through bouts of anger as I went through the divorce process and even afterwards. It's just one tool for me in my psychological self-care toolbox. I started using it whenever something trivial would anger or trigger me. The car that cut me off, no middle finger this time, I Rule, you get the I-R treatment and I move on with my day. My annoying neighbor complaining (again) about my cat walking through her yard - nope, you get the I-R too.

Not everything is irrelevant of course and some things need to be worked out or processed. I found that to make myself relevant, I needed energy and to save that energy for myself, I used the I-R.

If it works for you, by all means, use it. Different things work for different people. To get you started on your self-care journey and give yourself The Royal Treatment, use the checklist and follow-up questions below to recognize where stress may show up and what you can do to alleviate it.

The Royal Treatment Checklist

Becoming aware of the effect your personal and professional choices have on you is essential to helping you care for yourself. Think about how stress manifests in you and in your daily life, and how it keeps you from accomplishing great things within your kingdom. Feel free to add other signs that you are feeling over-worked, overextended, or overwhelmed. If you're not constantly curious about yourself, you may miss some important signs of stress — and I want more for you than that, Queen! If not addressed, that Keep Bucket is going to start to overflow again, which means you'll be right back where you started.

Warning Sign	Yes or No	If Yes, Describe the Effect on You
Increased anxiety or heightened worry	Yes ☐ No ☐	
Intrusive, negative thoughts and images that are difficult to shake	Yes ☐ No ☐	
Difficulty maintaining boundaries – work, life, other	Yes ☐ No ☐	
Having low or no energy	Yes ☐ No ☐	
Eating or sleeping too much or too little	Yes ☐ No ☐	
Regularly feeling angry and/or cynical	Yes ☐ No ☐	
Aches and pains or stomach/digestive issues	Yes ☐ No ☐	
Other	Yes ☐ No ☐	

Now that you've recognized how stress physically manifests, as well as its impact on you, assess your self-care practices.

Fortunately for you, Queen — many strategies are available to support self-care and reduce the signs and symptoms of stress. This exercise provides ideas about how to practice self-care across many areas of your life. Remember, Queen, that no one strategy works for everyone. So, try several until you find your favorites, and get the results you need.

How often do you find yourself doing the following?

Rate, using the following scale:

5-That's my Jam
4-Fairly Regularly
3-Rarely
2-Nope
1-What the Hell are You Even Talking About

Physical Self-Care	
	Eat regularly (e.g., breakfast and lunch)
	Make healthy food choices
	Get adequate sleep
	Exercise
	Get regular preventative medical care
	Get medical care when needed
	Take time off for your mental health
	Take time off when you are sick
	Make time for sex and intimacy
	Get massages or other body work
	Get your hair done
	Wear clothing that makes you feel good
	Spend time away from digital devices and social media
	Other:

Psychological Self-Care

	Make time for feeling grateful
	Make time for self-reflection
	Invest in therapy or coaching
	Journal
	Read literature unrelated to your work
	Learn a new skill or try a new activity
	Allow yourself to be curious
	Say "No" to extra responsibilities or things you don't need and/or want to do
	Spend time outdoors
	Spend time with others who bring out the best in you
	Engage in positive self-talk and reject negative self-talk
	Allow yourself to cry
	Other:

Spiritual Self-Care

	Make time for prayer, meditation, and/or reflection
	Spend time in silence
	Participate in a spiritual gathering, community, or group
	Take time to understand your purpose and place in the universe
	Other

Professional Self-Care

	Take time for breaks and eating lunch
	Take time to talk with coworkers
	Identify projects or tasks that are rewarding for you
	Pursue regular learning and professional development
	Negotiate for your value and needs
	Have a peer support group
	Other:

Let's continue Queens:

Now that you've assessed your self-care practices — let's get real.

What was the process of filling out the checklist like for you?

_____

_____

_____

_____

Were you surprised by any of your responses? If so, which ones?

_____

_____

_____

_____

In what areas are you strongest (more 4s and 5s)? Weakest (1s, 2s, 3s)?

_____

_____

_____

_____

What needs to change and what will you do to make these changes?

_____

_____

_____

_____

Chapter 11

Create Your Royal Riches

There's something to be said about a Queen who finds prosperity her way – and doesn't let a damn thing stop her from achieving her goals.

Take Empress Matilda for example. Back in the early 1100s, she was the daughter of King Henry I of England and had claim to the English throne. At a young age, she moved to Germany and married the future Holy Roman Emperor, Henry V. When her brother, Prince William, died, her father, the English King, pronounced her next in line. Back then, it was almost unheard of to have a woman sitting on the English throne.

Once her father died, there was a short coup (of course there was a coup, there can never not be a coup) and her cousin, Stephen of Blois, stole the crown (or earned it, that is contested). Matilda, known for her feistiness, was mad. She launched a campaign to take over the throne and ushered in a period of lawlessness and civil war known as "The Anarchy." I get goosebumps just thinking of it.

Needless to say, shit went down. One thing I wanted to call out is her determination for power, her people and their prosperity. Who knows what her motives were, but based on the choices she made, it was clear what she wanted. It's something we can all learn from.

When she was cornered at Oxford Castle in 1142 during a siege, she escaped by running away and crossing the frozen River Thames on foot. Now that's a rebel Queen if ever I heard of one! This woman pushed, struggled, and fought for what she wanted. In the end, she didn't get it – not the type of power she wanted – but she fought, and fought, and eventually found power through the legacy of her children.

In Matilda's case, she wanted power. And she fought hard to make it happen. In your case, it may be wealth, autonomy, fame, ease; you do you. Regardless, get into your Matilda mindset and prepare to do what it takes to achieve your dreams – because they're very much worth having.

Okay, back to business. Now, ladies, Matilda brought on anarchy to get what she wanted. For God's sake, please don't do that, but let's prepare you to fight for what you want.

You work hard every day for the riches and prosperity you're seeking. You follow the old-school idea of paying your dues, working your way up, making major sacrifices and finally reaching that C-level role only to realize that dream you've chased has come true – but it wasn't exactly what you were expecting. You've fought to earn money, but never once fought for creating money for yourself.

You're probably thinking, "Carrie-Ann, you've lost it. That's the same thing."

Wrong.

Earning money is work. It's trading your time and your effort for the almighty dollar. Sweat, stress, and time are exchanged for a paycheck (hopefully one with a well-deserved bonus attached). When earning money, there's a real quid pro quo there.

There's more magic in creating money. That's part of the reason I love the word "prosperity", which not only covers financial and material success, but also implies the side effects of success in overall health, wealth, and happiness.

Once I figured out the difference, I quit the "just get through the week" mentality about getting up and going to work. Instead, I felt more like a kid at a magic show, brimming with excitement about starting work each day. (I'm sure you're thinking, "Sounds nice, but how in the hell does that happen?") With patience, work, and creating what you are inspired to create, you are transforming your energy into prosperity. People will actually pay you to do what charges your batteries! Imagine that.

We have this idea that hard work has to be, well, hard. Difficult. A slog. The worst. And that is 100% not true. Consider the following example.

I had a client, let's call her Carol. Carol was a real overachiever. I mean the kind of person you'd beg and plead to help you with a project because you knew it would be done right. She was supersmart and capable. She had worked in the corporate world for quite some time, and then left to start her own consulting business. The business was new, less than two years old, yet she was growing at an amazing rate because of her reputation in her industry.

Carol had just been offered a contract that would earn her a great deal of money (more than double what she had ever made). It tapped directly into her area of expertise and wouldn't require a whole lot of work from her. It was, in a word "easy." And yet, she wasn't sure if she should take it.

This freaked Carol out. At the time, her husband had health problems and was having difficulty with work. Carol was the sole source of income for her family. They had just moved and didn't have a local support network of friends.

I was a little bit confused, at first, about why Carol would be freaked out by this opportunity. It seemed like the perfect job for her. It would take a lot off her plate and give her time to deal with the craziness at home. It would give her extra income to make up for the fact that her husband didn't have a job at the moment. What was the problem?

Then it dawned on me. I asked her, "What were your previous contracts like?"

"Oh God," Carol said. "Insanity. Crazy deadlines, unrealistic expectations, unappreciative leadership, wasted work, low pay. This is exactly why I left the last job in the first place to start my own thing. Now, that very same employer is begging me to work as a consultant from across the country at a higher rate and on my own terms."

"And they want you because of your expertise and training, right?" I asked.

"I guess."

"Bullshit," I laughed, appreciating our rapport and connection. "You know."

Carol laughed. "Okay. I know."

"You know or they wouldn't be begging you to do what you used to do for them, but now for more money and less stress. They specifically want you – all of you, expertise, experience, quality, attitude, all of it," I said. "So, here's what I'm thinking, Carol. The stress, the chaos, the feeling of being overworked, the lack of balance that you had for years – that's your comfort zone. It's what you're used to."

She paused and said, "Oh my God. That's it. If I'm not suffering, then I must not be working hard enough. What is wrong with me?"

Read that again slowly....

"If I'm not suffering, then I must not be working hard enough."

Sound familiar? It's no different than the common phrase "No Pain, No Gain" – and let's be frank. That phrase is complete garbage. Carol isn't the only one who has been conditioned along those lines, but Carol made a discovery. She found her inner saboteur – that part of your personality that deliberately tries to knock you down a peg. One that disrupts, delays, and otherwise hinders your success. Now that she knew what it was, she could put it to bed.

"There's nothing wrong with you, Carol," I replied. "It's what's happened to you – your training. You are living the life you were taught to live."

We talked for a long while after that, and for weeks to come before she got comfortable with where she was. This attitude was what she had learned and how she had been conditioned. It's what she learned from her parents, her culture, and from a toxic employer. If we're not fighting, sweating, or bleeding, then we're not working hard enough or doing our part. I'm going to bet at least one of you feels the same – and probably a whole hell of a lot more of you.

I said, "For just a moment, let's play. I want you to channel your inner white male. Let's go there. What would you do? What would you say to this opportunity?"

"I'd say I've already earned the right to sit back and take it easy and get money for nothing. I'd pull my shoulders back, stand up and straighten my pant legs, then head out for a cup of coffee."

We laughed, we were being a bit facetious, but it broke a barrier, and there was a lot of truth in it. That was how Carol woke up her inner leader – her Queen. She had earned the right to that contract, that crown, and, of course, she wasn't getting money for nothing.

She created this opportunity, this prosperity. She was no longer earning money. That part was done – she was creating money. She was getting paid for the years she had put in learning, getting her hands in the dirt, and sacrificing to get where she was. No one else could do what she had done. The information and talent she had in her bright, beautiful mind were worth what they were paying her. Perhaps it took her leaving and moving across the country for them to realize it, but they did, and now they were willing to put up the cash for it. She grabbed it with both hands while her Queen's Court cheered her on.

There is a story about Picasso that highlights this point. While the story is likely a legend, an "old wives' tale" as we should no longer be calling it, the story drives home the point. In the tale, a woman approaches Picasso in a restaurant after watching him scribble something on a napkin. She asks if she could have it. Picasso told her it would cost $10,000, or something along those lines. The woman was appalled and said, "But you did that in a matter of seconds. I watched you." to which Picasso replied, "No! It has taken me forty years to do that."

BOOM. Queen, it's all about you. You choose to create the life you want – so dammit, demand that you get paid for it!

A Go, or No-Go? That Is the Question.

Queen, do you feel as though you have to suffer in your work? Do you really want to work harder and not smarter? Remember, you're in charge of your decisions.

As I mentioned earlier, decisions can be complicated. You can make that process easier. While building my staffing company, I had to make decisions about whether or not to go after opportunities and commit to writing a proposal. Oftentimes, this is not an easy decision, given that many of the hours, weeks, even months spent on a proposal don't result in an award. That's part of business and equally a part of all other aspects of life. Not all efforts result in an amazing reward (Wouldn't it be magical if they did?) but we always learn something along the way. That said, I wanted to focus my time and that of my teams on worthwhile efforts. And I want the same for you.

A simple but powerful way that has worked for my clients is something I used in my business – a "Go or No-Go" decision-making process. This process is typically associated with the National Aeronautics and Space Administration (NASA) space program. After obvious investment and testing, the final decision to launch a spaceship comes down to a simple 'yes' or 'no' decision. Similarly, I want the decisions in your life to help launch you to greatness.

To aid your inner Queen in determining whether a choice is a Go or No-Go, it first needs to be aligned with your Core Values and your Vision. If it's not, it's a No-Go. If it is aligned, what are the more tactical things that are involved? It may be money or time, but it can be broken down into reasonable tasks.

The basic idea is that you make a list of criteria that go into the design of any project you take on. That project can be agreeing to sit on a charity board, taking on a work project, or agreeing to work with a particular client.

You take these criteria and see how they apply to each project you are taking on. For each criterion, you give a 'plus,' which means that this element lines up with your personal Values or Vision, or a 'minus,' which means that element does not line up with your personal Values or Vision. Easy-peasy.

Then, you add up the number of plusses and minuses you have at the end and see what the proportions are. If more of your answers are plusses, you can Go with confidence. If not, that's a No-Go. If it's close or a tie, ask more questions until you can make a decision.

Here's a sample of Go or No-Go criteria to give you a starting point:

CRITERIA	NOTES	+/-
Does this work/project/ relationship align with my values?		
Does this work/project/relationship fuel my Vision?		

CRITERIA	NOTES	+/-
Will this project make me want to jump out of bed?		
Am I passionate about this work?		
Do the client's Values align with mine?		
Does the client have the budget to finish the work?		
Will the scope and size of project work with my chosen velocity?		
What is the expected profit and is it aligned with what I know my time and energy is worth?		
Do I have the appropriate resources available, or will this make my "Keep" bucket overflow?		

This list above is, of course, just a suggestion. You can change the criteria to whatever fits you best. Hell, I have a friend who's created one for dating and includes questions such as "Am I equally attracted to him intellectually as I am physically? Does he have children and treat them well? Does he treat past wives/exes' with respect?" It really can be used for anything.

The idea, however, is that you have a list that fleshes out your Values and Vision for what types of projects, relationships, or choices you are going to take on. Whatever your Values, whatever your Vision, develop a set of criteria that will allow you to weigh the plusses and minuses of taking anything on before you decide Go or No-Go.

Chapter 12

An Edict from the Queen

We've already touched on Queen Victoria here – the strong woman who ruled the United Kingdom of Great Britain and Ireland for more than 63 years. She was intelligent, she was indestructible, and she knew how to say "No."

While most of us women have been taught to cower at the idea of saying "No" and disappointing others, Queen Victoria felt quite the opposite: "The important thing is not what they think of me, but what I think of them."

YES. Now that's the sort of strength I want from you. Whether you're a CEO of a Fortune 500 company, an overachieving mom managing the household, the sweet woman working the check-out counter or the Queen herself, "No" is a critical word in your vocabulary, so start using it. There are only 24 hours in the day, for all of us, and it's our call on how to spend those hours – no one else's.

Remember now, "No" is a complete sentence. It is one of the few exceptions to the subject-verb requirement for complete sentences and it sounds something like this:

- "Will you head up this project?" "No!"

127

- "Will you join this committee?" "No!"

- "Will you chaperone the field trip?" "No!"

- "Will you attend this gala?" "No!"

- "Please?" "No, No, a thousand times No."

Saying "No" when you feel like saying "No" is one of the most liberating things you can do for yourself. Say it out loud right now – provided you aren't sneaking in this chapter during a boring meeting. In that case, say it to yourself. "No, I will not be able to help you prepare that spreadsheet. Do it your damn self." Okay, cut out the last part of that in the interest of keeping your colleagues from turning into mean girls, but still.

Often, we feel obligated to do things simply because someone else asked us. The more you think about that, the more ridiculous it becomes. What right does someone have to impose obligations on us simply by asking? Why do I have to serve on a committee simply because you want me to?

I don't. And I won't.

Often, ego gets in the way. "Well," we think, "It's an honor to be asked. They wouldn't have asked me if they didn't think I would do a good job. They could have asked anyone, but they asked me. They need me. I will do a good job. No one else will do as good a job as I will. I can really make this the best it can be."

Blah blah blah. I've heard it all, sister, and I know, and you know, that sometimes those opportunities are just crap.

Maybe they asked you because you are convenient. Maybe they asked you because you have a reputation for saying "Yes" and that saves them the trouble of finding someone else. Maybe they asked you because you're easy to get along with.

There are a thousand reasons why they may have asked you. Some of them are very flattering, some of them are neutral, and some of them, quite frankly, are insulting. They may have asked you because they know you're a sucker and no one else wanted the job. You are above this, Queen!

Here's the thing – their motivations are irrelevant. (See – we're using that I-R already!)

The only thing that matters is your own personal motivation. What Value are you honoring by saying "Yes?" If the answer is none, the answer is "No!"

Are you agreeing to head up the committee because the work of the committee aligns with your Values? Are you committing your Queenly presence to go to the gala because you share a Vision with the fundraising goals? Are you consenting to sacrifice your valuable time by heading up this project because it increases your Velocity towards your own goals?

Queen, it's time for you to control your "Yesses" and your "Nos." A Queen knows when she does or doesn't want to be involved in something. In coaching, I call these my non-negotiables.

Let's talk about Jada for a second. She was a senior vice president that worked hard and made shit happen. She was energetic, positive, and inspiring – my kind of woman! Her boss, the only person above her, was not. Jada knew that, but she had worked with this particular woman for 10 plus years and followed her to various companies. Her Value of loyalty had been taken to an extreme and had become a saboteur.

Jada's boss had made a commitment to an oversight body that she and her team would produce an operations plan and budget that was 100% error free. The stress this standard of perfection put on Jada and her team was overwhelming.

We talked about leadership and the leader she wanted to be. Then we talked about the leaders she was willing to follow. Jada sought clarity about whether a job change was pending. I suggested that if she valued the relationship with her boss, then she needed to have a conversation with her about her non-negotiables. A bold conversation for sure, but Jada was ready to put on that crown. Her homework before our next session was to make that list of non-negotiables

Her first non-negotiable was, "I will not work in an environment where failure is not an option."

Coming to this conclusion was no small feat. Jada grew up in a family where perfection – from ironed clothing, to straight A's, to dating the "boy next door" – was the only option. She existed in a world where family problems were kept behind closed doors, and everyone was strong. She was conditioned to follow this way of thinking and continued to do so from one job to another.

In her 40s and now in an executive role, she was ready for a new choice. She appreciated her team and wanted them to be successful in both work and life and saw how the pressure was killing their spirits. She knew that team members would eventually leave. She was feeling that way herself.

Jada continued to write her list of non-negotiables and had that bold conversation with her boss. And the rules changed. Jada's inner Queen showed up, with full royal confidence, and demanded to be heard. Expectations changed and failures became opportunities.

Think about your own non-negotiables and then hold yourself accountable to your inner Queen by committing to them. This is when we look that part of us that was taught to be a pleaser right in the eyes and say, "No more." Your inner Queen is there to support you and she does not compromise on what is most important to you.

Don't Slay Dragons. Tame Them

Dragons show up in many ways. They may be bosses, friends, and often family. They could be behaviors we've put up with for too long. Sometimes we really do need to cut them from our lives but that's rare. More often, we need to tame those dragons by identifying what we will and will not tolerate — our non-negotiables — and then do exactly what the word implies: stop negotiating with ourselves and instead, create boundaries.

A fantastic resource for creating and respecting boundaries can be found by reading *Set Boundaries, Find Peace: A Guide to Reclaiming Yourself* by licensed therapist, New York Times bestselling author, and content creator, Nedra Glover Tawwab. Her Instagram account is an incredible resource on the topic, and I highly recommend that you follow her for great information on healthy boundaries and relationships.

So, what are your non-negotiables? What are the boundaries you need to create?

To help you get started, think of a non-negotiable you absolutely will not tolerate in your life – any part of your life.

- What makes you angry as a hornet or makes you want to punch a wall?

- What do you need and what can you not live without?

Come up with five or more non-negotiables – ways to tame those dragons – for all areas of your life and keep them close. Sometimes, we need reminders; keeping your non-negotiables in clear view will help.

Mine are posted on the wall next to my computer, along with dozens of other stickies. It might work for you to have them as a note on your phone, or as part of the wallpaper on your computer, or maybe a note on the mirror in your bathroom.

The point is that we all need constant reminders, and a visual that we come across multiple times a day is a good idea. I'm not perfect and I know that. I don't expect perfection of myself which is why I have all of these sticky notes – but what I do expect is that each day I wake up, breathe deeply, dust off my royal mantle (what a Queen wears to her coronation), and get ready to shake up my nation. Because in the end, it's the Queen's call. And today, I wear the crown.

Chapter 13

Determine Your Royal Decree

Queen, hold that head up high – you've made it!

You showed up, put in the work and you earned that stunning, stellar crown on your head. It's shiny and sparkling, or dark and dramatic, (You do you!) and shows everyone in the world what you are capable of and who you are: perfect, insanely beautiful inside and out and not a woman to be messed with. I am so proud of you. And most important, I bet you're damn proud of yourself, too.

As someone who has been there before, I cannot express how joyful it feels to start celebrating you, your life story, and your enduring commitment to ensure you remain a priority in your life!

The fact that you connected with me personally, or picked up this book, was your first sign that it was time for some work on "you." Now that you've put in the hours and set the plan in motion, how do you feel? Jot that down – quickly!

In our lives, these moments of immense fulfillment and happiness are precious. So, savor them!

Over the course of this book, you've put a lot of work into yourself – ranging from mental to emotional work, maybe even physical work – and that is not something to be taken lightly.

You put yourself first, you persevered, and you're creating the life you want for yourself – as long as you continue to take care of yourself. Queens cannot achieve success without a wonderful, diamond-worthy self-care regimen, after all.

Our last bit of work together is Writing and Declaring Your Royal Decree – the announcement that summarizes what is most important to you and your Vision for your kingdom and your life. It's your bold-ass, no-apology, this is me announcement to the world and a reminder to yourself. So run over and grab those notes from the exercises you've completed!

This Royal Decree will allow you to step into your role with the confidence needed to rule your kingdom. It will include your Values and Vision. These are foundational to achieving your regal purpose and fueling your passions. When it comes to Velocity, you decide on the exercises and tools that will keep you going and enable you to achieve full prosperity.

After my Values and Vision, my decree includes the Velocity tools that work the best for me. This includes the roles I play (chapter 7). That list reminds me that I am so many incredible things and that I can show up at any time as any of them, and that those not in the forefront at any given moment are still there in the background supporting me. I keep my non-negotiables on my decree (chapter 12) and when I start to feel stress in my life, I go back and check my choices against them along with my Values. I have an image of the word IR|Relevant (chapter 10). I use the other exercises as well, but those I've included on my Decree are the ones that resonate most for me. What works for you?

To get you started, I've created a template you can use. You can download it for free at my website, www.queensdecree.com or create your own. You're in charge Queen.

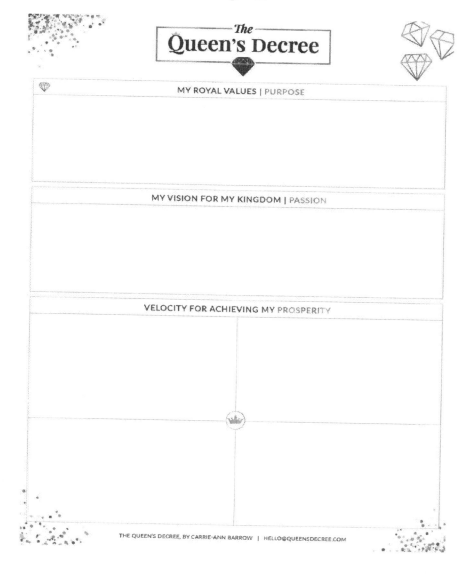

The

Queen's Decree

MY ROYAL VALUES | PURPOSE

MY VISION FOR MY KINGDOM | PASSION

VELOCITY FOR ACHIEVING MY PROSPERITY

THE QUEEN'S DECREE, BY CARRIE-ANN BARROW | HELLO@QUEENSDECREE.COM

This Royal Decree shouts from the mountain-top that you are in charge of your kingdom!

Consider hosting a dinner with your closest friends to celebrate your Royal Decree and what this means to you! Post it to your social media. This is news-worthy, my love. This may also help you bring out the royal in others!

From One Queen to Another

Dear Queen – you are amazing. You are beautiful. You are in charge of your choices, and I am grateful that you have allowed me to be a part of your journey. Continue it. Build that dream. Build Your Kingdom.

If you enjoyed this book or found it useful, I would be extremely grateful if you'd post a short review on Amazon or social media. Your support really does make a difference. I am committed to reading all the reviews personally.

Thank you, Queen for your support. I am honored to have been a part of your kingdom.

Carrie-Ann Barrow

About The Author

Carrie-Ann Barrow coaches women from aspiring entrepreneurs to founders and executives, helping them clarify their visions and find fulfillment in work and in life. A successful entrepreneur who built and sold multiple businesses and made Washingtonian magazine's list of Women to Watch, Carrie-Ann brings insights from both her professional and her personal life.

The first woman in her family to attend college, Carrie-Ann battled challenges from a young age. She persevered, gave up the things that didn't serve her, and decided to live for herself. Now, Carrie-Ann, supports others as they focus on what makes them the best version of themselves, without apologizing, and find fulfillment. She equips her clients with practical frameworks, strategies, and tools to make real progress and see meaningful results.

With a boldly authentic approach merging honesty, openness, humor, and positivity, she shifts seamlessly from coach to consultant to confidant, showing up in the way her clients need her.

Carrie-Ann is a voice of perseverance committed to empowering women to design their own destinies.

Learn more about Carrie-Ann at queensdecree.com

Printed in Great Britain
by Amazon

36877558R00079